Fishing In Oregon's

DESCHUTES RIVER

Fishing in Oregon's
DESCHUTES RIVER

Scott Richmond

Flying Pencil Publications
Scappoose, Oregon

© 1993 by Four Rivers Press, Inc.
Illustrations © 1992 by Four Rivers Press, Inc.
Maps © 1993 by Flying Pencil Publications

Published by Flying Pencil Publications in collaboration with Four Rivers Press. Address all inquiries to:
Flying Pencil Publications
33126 Callahan Road
Scappoose, Oregon 97056
503-543-7171

Photographs by Scott Richmond unless credited otherwise. Maps by Madelynne Diness Sheehan and Lynn Kertell. Line drawings by Lora Crestwick. Cover art by Vic Erickson. Book and cover design by John Laursen.

Printed in the United States of America

10 9 8 7 6 5 4 3 2 1

Library of Congress Catalog Card Number: 93-70651

ISBN: 0-916473-08-2

To the wild fish of Oregon

Acknowledgments

Mike McLucas for the Foreword, review of the manuscript, and general advice and information about the river. Lora Crestwick for the line drawings, some of which appeared previously in *The Pocket Gillie*. Madelynne Diness Sheehan for maps and editing. John Laursen for book and cover design. Vic Erickson for cover art. Randy Stetzer for review and some photos. Jed Davis for advice on spinner fishing for steelhead. Rick Hafele for advice on hatch charts. Lynn Ewing for review. Bill Bakke of Oregon Trout for review. Randall Kaufmann for flies used in Chapter 8. And especially my wife Barbara, who believes in my projects, mostly.

The following people and agencies provided helpful information and review of certain portions of the manuscript: Karen Perault and Ed Perault of the Bureau of Land Management, Steve Pribyl and Pat Wray of the Oregon Department of Fish and Wildlife, Jim Griggs and Mark Fritsh of the Confederated Tribes of Warm Springs, Jacque Greenleaf of Oregon State Parks and Recreation Department, Bill Rydblom of Oregon State Marine Board, Carl Rhodes of Oregon State Police.

Contents

Maps and Charts

Foreword

By Mike McLucas

The first step to increasing our enjoyment of an object or an experience is to gain a better understanding of it. This is particularly true of Oregon's Deschutes River. It is both an object, which you can view and savor, and an experience as you fish and boat its waters.

The more you understand this unique river resource and how you relate to it, the more you will enjoy it. For example, it is great fun to go fishing. However, the experience is enhanced if, in some measure, you understand the fish and the world they live in.

Mike McLucas has guided fishing trips on the Deschutes River for over 20 years. His family has owned The Oasis Resort in Maupin since 1955. Mike has been deeply involved in recreation management issues on the Deschutes.

Years ago I authored a short piece for *Fishing In Oregon* entitled "The Deschutes—Love It or Leave It Alone." I still feel that way about the Deschutes. As river use increases, I put my faith in what you might call Mike's Law of Resource Use:

Information and Understanding lead to appreciation and enjoyment.

Appreciation and Enjoyment lead to respect and caring.

Respect and Caring lead to even deeper appreciation and (most important of all) to commitment to stewardship.

I hope you will use this book to fit yourself into that equation and advance yourself to stewardship. I especially encourage your attention to the first two chapters on ethics and personal conduct. As more and more people use and enjoy the Deschutes, these considerations become paramount.

You don't need to speak Latin or have a degree from MIT to understand this book. You will gain insights that will help you successfully ply the Deschutes in search of wild trout and steelhead. You will benefit from Scott's common sense explanation of "why" and "how" these fish respond (or not!) to your efforts. And most importantly his genuinely informed, but modest (and lightly humorous) style will welcome you to the family of Deschutes lovers—and guide you toward active participation as a river steward.

Maupin, Oregon
March, 1993

First Casts

The Deschutes River is one of the crown jewels of Oregon. It has a blue-ribbon rainbow trout fishery, and its summer steelheading is among the best anywhere. If that were not enough, its rapids attract whitewater enthusiasts from around the country. All this in a river resource that is only two hours from a major population center.

This book has two purposes. One is to help recreationists of all types—but especially anglers—get the most out of their Deschutes River experience. The second purpose is to give all river users the information they need to protect the resource from damage, so we can all continue to enjoy the pleasures it has to offer.

The Deschutes is a popular river used by many people with diverse interests. By following a few simple guidelines, everyone's enjoyment of the river will be increased. "People" conflicts will be minimized, as will ignorant abuse of the river environment. This is the thrust of the first two chapters. Chapter 1 covers river etiquette, and Chapter 2 addresses subjects such as camping, private property, water, and personal hygiene.

The overview map shows how to get to the Deschutes River from major highways in Oregon and southern Washington. Chapters 3 through 6 give detailed driving directions to specific places on the river, as well as describe the campgrounds and recreation sites in that area. Both drive-in and boat-in camps are covered. For convenience, the chapters correspond to normal river drifts or drive-in trips. Each chapter has road maps and river maps for the area being discussed.

Details about fishing the Deschutes are presented in Chapters 7 through 9. The first of these covers subjects of common interest to all anglers: fishing regulations and permits, fish species likely to be caught, wading the river, and releasing fish. Fishing for trout is discussed in detail in Chapter 8. Here you will find out how to locate trout in the Deschutes, how to present your fly to them, and what fly to tie on. Since

---

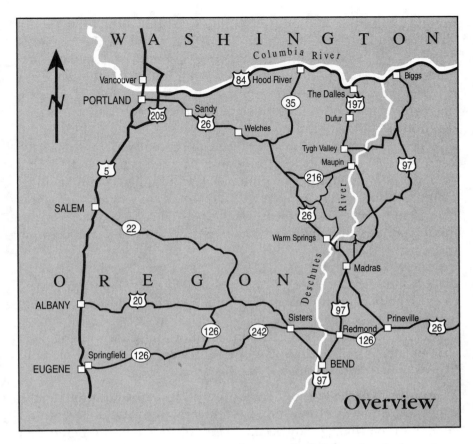

Overview

90% of the trout fishing on the Deschutes is fly fishing, that is the primary focus of this chapter. However, there is a section at the end for those using spinning gear.

Fishing for Deschutes steelhead is covered in Chapter 8, and both fly and hardware angling are discussed. Subjects that are covered include proper gear for steelhead fishing, how to find the fish, and how to chose a fly or lure.

Services in the region that are of interest to recreationists are listed in Chapter 10.

Who Owns the River? Many governmental agencies are involved in the management of the Deschutes River, including the Bureau of Land Management (BLM), the Confederated Tribes of the Warm Springs Reservation (CTWS), Oregon State Parks and Recreation Department, Oregon Department of Fish and Wildlife (ODFW). There is additional involvement from the Oregon State Police, the counties of Wasco, Sherman, and Jefferson, the Oregon State Marine Board, the Bureau of Indian Affairs. Throw in private landowners, commercial outfitters and guides, private rafters, powerboaters, sport fishers, wildlife watchers, a railroad or two, and quite a few others. Now try to get them all to agree on anything and coordinate their efforts. The marvel is that anything gets done at all.

The managing agencies and private and commercial interests have been involved in a years-long, federally mandated effort to develop a comprehensive plan for managing the Deschutes River area. The final plan was published in early 1993. Two things are guaranteed by this plan. One is that it will not please everyone. That's the way it is with political processes; they involve compromises, and no one gets everything they want.

The other guarantee is that this book will always be a little bit out of date. No matter when we go to press, something will change on the river as the plan is implemented. Therefore, recreationists need to be alert to changes in rules and regulations, campsites, etc. Read all signs as you travel on and near the river, because things are going to change a lot over the next three years. You may obtain a copy of the Management Plan from BLM and anticipate those changes.

My Approach to the River. I admit to few biases in river use, as long the user is not abusive. However, I have several personal preferences. I generally travel light, partly because I enjoy living unencumbered, and partly because I believe it's easier on the land. Besides, I often travel alone and have no one to help me carry a lot of gear up the bank to a campsite.

I own both a drift boat and a raft, and I use both on the Deschutes. Therefore, all camps and points of interest are presented from the view of one who is drifting the river, rather than proceeding up it in a powerboat.

My apologies to powerboaters, who can use this book to find camps only if they motor downstream. I don't own a jet boat, so I don't have that perspective of the river. While I have no strong personal prejudices or religious feelings against powerboats, I find them to be expensive and possessing an engine. Boat engines and I view each other with mutual suspicion, each expecting and receiving abuse at the hands of the other.

My preferred approach to trout and steelhead is with a fly rod, however I try not to be a pompous ass about it. I fish with other techniques, and I feel that any serious angler can learn something from a skilled angler of differing persuasion. When I fly fish, I have no preference for either dry flies or wets, and I use whatever I think the fish want at the moment.

I release all trout caught in the Deschutes, and the larger the trout the better I feel about letting it go. I release all wild steelhead, but generally keep a few hatchery fish for the dining table.

Thankfully, I passed the point of fishing blood-lust some years back. I like to test my skill on the river, but a brace of trout well stalked and cast to, or a single wild steelhead from a new run I discovered on my own mean more to me than dozens of fish hooked otherwise.

Often, I am content to put my rod aside and lie on the bank propped on one elbow. I watch the river slip past, think of all that lives in and around the water, and let the river wash away the shallow pretensions and have-to's of modern life. I soak up the smell of sage and juniper, admire the way grass trembles with dry stiffness in a breeze I cannot feel, and listen to the four-part harmony of rushing water—the tenors of twin riffles, the baritone of standing waves, and the percussive bass of surging current in deep water. Moments like this are part of the experience of fishing the Deschutes River, and it may be that they are the finest part because they awaken the desire to understand the river better and to treat it with care and respect.

Other Resources. Some other resources of value to Deschutes-bound recreationists are:

Handbook to the Deschutes River Canyon, by James Quinn, et al. This is the standard whitewater reference book for the canyon. It was first published in 1979. It has been reprinted several times, but the content has remained unchanged. Therefore some of the information—especially that on campsites and use of the river—is out of date or missing. Also, the drift miles below Maupin are off by about one half mile, and so they do not correspond with those in this book or with the river miles shown on maps of the area. However, most of the guidelines for running rapids are still valid.

Deschutes, by Dave Hughes, is a "coffee table" book of river photos and text. It is a well-written, visually pleasing summary of both the human and natural history of the canyon. It gives the best "feel" for the river of any book available.

Lower Deschutes River, by Esther Appel, is a topographical river map that will save you the cost of buying several USGS topos. *Lower Deschutes River Public Lands* is a map published by the Bureau of Land Management. It is not as detailed as a topo map, but it shows more of the surrounding area. It also shows public vs. private land ownership.

Spinner Fishing for Steelhead, Salmon, and Trout, by Jed Davis, is the best reference on fishing with spinners.

Western Hatches, by Rick Hafele and Dave Hughes, and *Aquatic Insects and Their Imitations,* by Rick Hafele and Scott Roderer, are both excellent sources of information about the aquatic critters imitated by flyfishers. Both include fly patterns suitable for the Deschutes.

Flies: The Best One Thousand, by Randy Stetzer, and *The Fly Tyer's Nymph Manual* and *Tying Dry Flies* by Randall Kaufmann, are my favorite sources of fly patterns. Both authors have spent years guiding on the Deschutes, and their experience is reflected in the patterns they present.

Fishing in Oregon, by Madelynne Diness and Dan Casali, is a complete guide to all fishing waters in the state. It gives a good overview of other rivers and lakes that you might want to visit while in the Deschutes area.

The Pocket Gillie (Flyfishing Essentials), by Scott Richmond, is a vest-pocket handbook for fly fishers of all abilities. It gives details on aspects of fly fishing that are only briefly touched on in this book. Take it with you when you fish the rivers and lakes of North America, and use it to help you locate receptive trout, choose the right fly, and present it with confidence.

1

Ethics and Etiquette

When we fish the Deschutes or camp on its banks, we are participating in a complex ecosystem of water, plants, trees, birds, reptiles, mammals, insects, fish of several species, people, and even soil and rocks. All these elements are intricately linked in a web of dependency. We each have a responsibility to educate ourselves about the issues concerning this ecosystem, and to work for its preservation and improvement.

The Deschutes has special regulations for fishing, camping, boating, and fire use; some of these are listed in other chapters of this book. These regulations are for the protection of the river resource, as well as to ensure equitable sharing of the river by recreationists.

However, if good manners were limited to the letter of the law, everyone's enjoyment of the river would suffer. There is a code of etiquette on the Deschutes that should be followed for the greater enjoyment of all. The best advice for behavior on and around the river is the Golden Rule: "Do unto others as you would have them do unto you," where "others" includes the entire ecosystem. Besides this general rule, here are a few specific guidelines.

If someone is fishing near an area you want to fish, ask if you will disturb them. If they are sitting, and not fishing, they may be resting the water or waiting for the light to change. In either case, ask before you fish.

Don't be a hole hog: don't monopolize the good water for long periods. Give someone else a chance.

If someone is fishing a run for steelhead they are probably working their way downstream, especially if they are fly fishing. Don't wade into the river below them, or near them upstream. If you are not sure how far downstream they are going, and you want to fish the water, ask first. Generally, you should stay at least 150 yards from them. This gives enough room to hook and play a fish upstream from someone, and rests the water for about an hour between anglers.

Manners are contagious. Which kind do you want to perpetuate on the river?

If you are in a boat or raft, give bank anglers a wide berth. Notice where they are casting to, and give them lots of space. If you aren't sure what water they are fishing, ask them. Try to stay at least 30 feet away from the water they are fishing, and pass by quietly without splashing or making other noise that will be transmitted through the water.

Don't pull your boat or raft into a backeddy until you are sure no one is fishing it.

Clear out of launching/landing sites quickly. Be prepared so you can launch quickly and be out of other people's way. If the ramp can accommodate two boats, stay to one side so someone else can use it, too.

When drifting the river in a large group with several boats, stay close together so you don't spread across the width of the river.

When passing through rapids, leave at least 50 yards between you and the craft in front of you.

There are basic boating right-of-way rules, such as: down-river-bound traffic has the right-of-way; and boats should bear to the right when meeting. However, once a powerboat is in a rapids it cannot back down, and drift craft need to wait to enter the rapids until the power boat is clear. At the same time, a powerboat should not enter a rapids if

Some boat ramps can accommodate two boats at once. Stay to one side, like this considerate boater, so others can use the ramp, too.

a drift craft is already in it or is about to enter it.

Powerboaters need to be aware of the affect of their wake as they pass drift craft and bank anglers.

Boaters of all persuasions should recognize the right of boaters of differing persuasions to use the river.

Don't abuse the riparian zone, the thin strip of vegetation along the river. This zone is crucial habitat to all life, both in and along the river. Examples of abuse are: breaking down trees

Pack out all trash. There is a dispenser of free plastic trash bags near Davidson Flat.

and brush to get to a favored campsite from the river (use an established trail instead); camping in a grassy area when an established campsite is nearby (use the established camp); nailing boards to trees for a kitchen shelf (bring a fold-up table). Islands are especially important ecologically. Therefore, camping is not permitted on them, and extreme care should be taken when visiting one.

Dispose of human waste properly. Personal hygiene has gotten to be a major problem on the river. Some popular flats are beginning to look and smell more like stockyards than campgrounds. Relieve yourself, but don't leave a visual, malodorous, and sanitary problem for others. See Chapter 2 for specific guidelines.

Don't litter. All established drive-in campgrounds have garbage cans. Use them. Only one boat-in site has garbage cans, so boaters need to pack out what they pack in. If you are drifting the upper part of the river, garbage bags are available near Davidson Flat. See Chapter 2 for more guidelines on garbage and cooking clean up.

Leave an area looking better than you found it. If you see bottles, cans, or other trash, pick them up and dispose of them. This is a contagious habit. Once you start doing it, others will follow your example. BLM and other land managers have found that tidy, well-maintained campsites tend to stay that way. They have also found the converse to be true.

Keep dogs and other pets under control. If they tend to wander, use a leash and tie them up in camp. Many canyon game birds nest from June through August, so prevent your dog from roaming at large during this period. Anytime you tie a pet and leave camp for a while, make sure it has shade and water. Animals can easily die when exposed to temperature extremes, even for short periods of time. Think ahead: if you tie your dog where it is in the shade now, will it still have shade when you come back?

Firearms cannot be discharged in the Deschutes River corridor (on the river, or up to a quarter mile from the riverbank) from the third Saturday in May to August 31.

2

Being There

Enjoy your visit to the Deschutes River canyon. Relax, run the rapids, catch some fish, catch some rays. This chapter offers guidelines for your present enjoyment of the river and its environment, as well as recommendations for participation in the on-going effort to ensure future enjoyment of the river by everyone.

Every person who visits the Deschutes canyon has some impact on its natural environment, and some of that impact is negative. Fortunately, the natural environment has prodigious self-healing energies, and if the negative impact of people visiting the canyon is low, then this self-healing capability can repair most of the damage. But if the damage is too great for the canyon world to repair itself, then each year it will become at little more degraded until we finally wake up and realize what has been lost. The guidelines in this chapter are aimed at minimizing the impact of people on the canyon, as well as the impact of people on other people.

Some of these guidelines are regulations enforced by law. Some of these regulations are enforced all year, some are seasonal, and others are imposed to deal with changing circumstances. Recreationists in the Deschutes canyon need to be alert to changes in the regulations and read all posted signs; things may have changed since your last visit.

Camping in the Deschutes River Canyon

Camping in the Deschutes canyon is "primitive." Few of the drive-in sites have drinking water, and many of the boat-in sites don't even have an outhouse. Therefore, campers need to be self-sufficient and prepared to take care of themselves. For many people, this is part of the appeal of camping here. The freedom from civilized encumbrances puts one in better touch with the natural world, and from this contact comes self-discovery and renewal.

There are over 30 drive-in campgrounds and recreation sites on the lower Deschutes River. In addition to the drive-in campgrounds, there are over 50 camps that can be reached only by boat, foot, or bike.

Drive-in Camps and Recreation Sites. Drive-in campgrounds fall into two broad categories: developed campgrounds and semi-developed campgrounds.

Developed campgrounds are usually large with designated campsites, most of which have a table. These campgrounds often have drinking water, have adequate parking, good roads, are suitable for RVs (although only Maupin City Park has RV hookups), and have a boat launch. The developed campgrounds are Trout Creek, Maupin City Park, Beavertail, Macks Canyon, and Deschutes River State Park.

Semi-developed campgrounds have an outhouse, garbage cans, a few scattered tables (maybe), sometimes a rough boat launch, and sometimes a waste water sump. In these campgrounds, you should camp in previously established tent sites. Sometimes the roads leading into these campgrounds are rocky and have large chuck holes.

Recreation sites are areas where you may park a car or launch a boat, but where camping is not permitted or is difficult.

Boat-in Camps. Unless there are signs stating otherwise, you may camp anywhere you want on public land. However, in this fragile environment it is best to camp in established sites, preferably with an outhouse, so as to minimize impact.

The campsites that are listed in this book are the ones that have an outhouse, or that are large and well-established. In addition, a few small sites are listed for long stretches of the river with no other type of camp.

Not all boat-in sites have a name, although if a name is in common use it is mentioned here. Both the river mile (measured from the confluence with the Columbia), and drift mile (beginning at the boat ramp at Warm Springs) are shown for each campsite. There is a description of how to recognize the campsite as you drift downstream, and the campsite itself is described.

Boat-in sites have no facilities other than an outhouse, and many sites do not have an outhouse.

While the Deschutes generally flows north, it has many twists and turns, and at any point the river may be flowing north, east, west, and sometimes even a little south. Therefore, terms like "west bank" and "east bank" do not refer to actual compass directions. In this book, the following conventions are used for east, west, left, and right: If you are headed **downstream**, and are facing **forward** (normal rowing position in a drift craft), "east bank" is on your right and "west bank" is on your left.

Where to Camp. In the developed campgrounds—Deschutes River State Park, Beavertail, Macks Canyon, Maupin City Park, and Trout Creek—camping should be in designated campsites. However, on all other public land you may camp wherever you want, with the exception of islands, where camping is not allowed. Also, camping is not permitted on Reservation lands except at Dry Creek, where a Warm Springs permit is required (see Chapter 7).

Although "pristine" campsites are an attraction, it is usually better to stay in a well used campsite and leave other areas untouched. This way the environmental damage is concentrated, and other areas are left for wildlife and aesthetic enjoyment. If possible, pick a site away from the riverbank so you will not disturb the riparian zone. The riparian zone is the narrow strip of vegetation along the river bank, and is crucial to a thriving community of fish and wildlife.

Wherever possible, camp where an outhouse is convenient. Large groups should always camp in areas that have an outhouse. Regardless of where you camp, you must keep your automobile on established roads and off vegetation.

Not all drive-in sites are suitable for trailers and RVs. The State Park can accommodate RVs, but there are no hookups. The Maupin City Park, however, has full RV hookups for a fee.

When you pack-up your camp, leave no trace that you were there. On the lower part of the river some people have nailed boards onto live trees in order to build a cooking shelf. This practice can lead to a premature death of the trees, which is ironic since the trees were the reason people camped there. Another destructive practice is digging ditches around tents. The desert environment is fragile, and holes and ditches are an invitation to erosion. The only time to dig a hole is for human waste

This camper has wisely pitched a tent on ground that has already been well used, rather than on un-trampled grass.

or waste water, and these should be covered up when you are done with them.

The managing agencies on the river are beginning a campsite rehabilitation program. They will close some sites (posting signs to that effect) either temporarily or permanently. Lists of closed sites will be available from BLM, ODFW, and State Parks.

Limits on length of stay and number of people. BLM has specific rules for length of stay at any one campsite. These are:

No more than 14 days out of any 28 in all drive-in campgrounds.

No more than five days in boat-in sites. You must vacate a site for four days before re-occupying it.

These rules apply to all your gear, whether you are staying with it or not. When you move, everything must go. At boat-in sites you cannot establish a new camp within a quarter mile of your previous camp.

The State Park at the mouth has a length-of-stay rule of no more than 10 days out of 14. Dry Creek has a maximum stay of 10 consecutive days. Some boat-in sites on the lower river have an experimental voluntary 24-hour limit. This is intended to ease conflicts between users.

In 1993 a new rule was established to limit the number of people in both commercial and non-commercial groups. These limits are:

From the Locked Gate to Sherars Falls, 24 people or less.

Elsewhere, 16 people or less.

Fees. Neither BLM nor the State charge for day use of public campgrounds and picnic areas, however they do charge for overnight use of drive-in campgrounds. At this time, the following fees are in effect.

The BLM fee is $3.00 per night for all drive-in campgrounds, plus $1.00 for each additional vehicle. There is no charge for boat-in sites. There are now fee stations at all named campgrounds.

The State Park charges $9.00 per night.

There is no fee for camping at Dry Creek, however a Warm Springs permit is required for each family unit.

The Maupin City Park has full RV hookups for $12.00 per night. Tent camping is $6.00 per day for one vehicle and up to six persons. Additional vehicles are $4.00 per day, and additional people are $1.00 per day. There are senior citizen discounts.

BLM charges $3.00 per night for camping, plus $1.00 for an additional vehicle. Fee stations are located at all BLM campgrounds.

Tips About Driving Deschutes Roads

Some of the roads are quite rough, with large dips and potholes, so you might not want to take the family Ferrari down them. Make sure your car has adequate clearance for the roads and turn-offs you are driving. The service stations in Maupin do a brisk trade repairing the bottom 12 inches of cars belonging to drivers whose enthusiasm exceeded their judgment. Here are some other tips.

Go slowly on the rough roads—20 miles an hour, or less. It's better for your car, and better for the road. Some stretches are suitable only for 10 mph. From Maupin south to the Locked Gate, the speed limit is 20 mph. If more people drove at that speed (or less) the road would not deteriorate as fast. From Maupin to Sherars, the speed limit on the paved road is 35 mph. Below Sherars, the road to Macks Canyon has a 20 mph speed limit.

Don't be in too much of a hurry on gravel roads. OK, so you want to

Park off the road so others may pass safely.

be the first one to that prime fishing hole. Just remember, gravel is great stuff when you are going straight ahead, but it is slippery when you brake or turn. Stopping on gravel takes much longer than on pavement, and turns cannot be taken as fast. Many roads develop a washboard surface that can throw you into a skid if you turn with too much speed. Don't brake hard and turn at the same time; you could find your car skidding on all four tires . . . or maybe the roof.

Park far enough off the road so others may pass safely, but don't get too close to the edge since the road bank sometimes caves in.

Be sure you have a usable spare tire for your vehicle. If you are pulling a trailer, have a spare tire for it, too.

Fasten your seat belt.

Keep vehicles out of riparian areas. Stay at least 50 feet from the river, if at all possible.

Some rural roads leading to the Deschutes make sharp 90-degree turns as they go around section corners and property boundaries. Be alert, or you could find yourself in the middle of a well-plowed field or a herd of cows.

Use a lower gear when going down steep hills, in order to save your brakes.

Check your tires after driving the rough access roads; you may have lost a lot of air. Also, take a quick look at your exhaust system; your muffler may be hanging by a thread.

Watch for deer on the roads, especially at dawn and just after dusk. They can be quite thick along the river and on SR 216 west of Pine Grove.

Don't drive on grassy areas or other vegetation.

Slow down when passing a campground along a gravel or dirt road. This will help keep the camping areas from getting dusty.

If a gate was closed when you got to it, make sure you close it immediately after passing through.

Getting gas late at night can be a problem. Between Madras and Portland, there are few gas stations that stay open late. Sometimes there is an all-night station open at Government Camp, but not always. Early and late season can be especially nerve-wracking for those who forgot to gas-up earlier in the day. At these times of year, the Maupin stations shut down at 6 PM, and most other stations between Sandy and Madras close at 9 PM or 10 PM. As of this writing, the Oasis Resort in Maupin pumps gas until the cafe closes at 11 PM, but it is closed from November through March.

Private Property *vs.* Public Property

The lower Deschutes River is a National Wild and Scenic River and an Oregon State Scenic Waterway. Many people believe that means that all the riverbank is public property. In fact, there are large sections of riverbank that are in private hands. In addition, there are several areas where the land is privately owned, but public access is permitted by the owner with some restrictions.

Users of the river need to be observant of all property rights. They need to respect "No Trespassing" signs where they are posted, and to "tread lightly" on private land to which they are allowed access.

BLM has published a map titled "Lower Deschutes River Public Lands" which shows the divisions between public and private land. It is available at several places, including the District Office in Prineville. Recreationists should be aware, however, that land often changes hands, and the ownership shown on the BLM map is approximate.

What Is Trespassing? The legal issues about ownership of the Deschutes River bottom are murky. What is described here reflects how trespass is currently enforced by the Oregon State Police.

Ownership of the river *bank* is divided among federal, state, private, and tribal owners. The boundary of the Warm Springs Reservation extends to mid-river, so for the 31 miles of river that borders the Reservation, the river bottom is part of the Reservation. This means, for example, that you may not anchor a boat or fish off a gravel bar west of mid-river in this area. The only exception is the six miles below Dry Creek, where a permit is required (see Chapter 7). It also means that all islands west of mid-river along the Reservation border belong to the CTWS. These are posted for no trespassing.

All islands on the east side of the river are public property, however camping on them is prohibited due to their fragile ecology.

River bottom rights are complicated and not fully resolved in the rest

Islands west of mid-river along the boundary of the Warm Springs Reservation, are part of the Reservation. To protect the important ecology of these islands, they are posted for no trespassing by the Confederated Tribes of Warm Springs (CTWS).

of the river, but in general, as long as you are on the river, or walking along its bottom (but still in the river) you are not trespassing. However, if you tie your boat to an overhanging tree, or pull it up on the beach, or walk the riverbank where there is private property posted with "No Trespassing" signs—you are vulnerable to arrest and prosecution.

Private Land with Public Access. There are many areas where the land is privately owned, but the owner has generously granted public access, sometimes with limited rights. For instance, the heavily used boat landing at Harpham Flat is owned by the CTWS, as is the popular take-out at Sandy Beach. Also, there is one mile of riverbank between Mecca Flat and Trout Creek that is owned by the Luelling family. Here you may fish, walk, ride a bike, land a boat, and generally enjoy yourself on the riverbank, but you may not camp, shoot a gun, or litter on their property. Another area of public access is the road between the Locked Gate and North Junction. Parts of this road are privately owned by the Deschutes Club. They allow public walk-ins (no bikes, etc.), which lets people reach the public land that is upstream of the Locked Gate. (Within the first seven miles above the Locked Gate, about half the riverbank is publicly owned. The remaining six miles to North Junction is all private property.)

Another major piece of private land is the railroad tracks. Many people walk along the Burlington Northern tracks to reach their favorite fishing spots. Some sections of track are posted for no trespassing, and Burlington Northern has the right to prosecute. Recreationists should recognize that this is, in fact, private property. If they choose to walk the tracks, they should be alert to approaching trains and maintenance equipment, and be aware that the trains do not run on a set schedule. And, it should be needless to say, walking across the trestles is very dangerous.

The public should understand that access to private lands is a privilege granted by the owners. We are guests on their property. If the owners find their property being abused by a few irresponsible or ignorant people, they may make the land off-limits to everyone. Some ways that the land can be abused are: camping where camping is not permitted; cutting down trees; building fires when not allowed; leaving gates open which had been closed; damaging fences; harassing livestock; littering and dumping garbage; hunting where it is not permitted.

Public access to private land is a privilege. Heed all restrictions.

Dealing with a Desert Climate

The Deschutes River flows through a desert canyon. This is a different environment than most people are used to. Here are a few things you should be aware of.

The arid desert climate can be hard on your skin, especially your hands. If they are in and out of the water a lot, they can get chapped and cracked fast. You may want to take along some kind of skin moisturizer.

Take along lots of sunscreen, preferably the waterproof kind. You can be burned quickly by the sun, especially when it is reflecting off the water. Put sunscreen on in the morning, and reapply throughout the day. Noon is a good time to reapply sunscreen.

Be prepared for temperature extremes. At night you may lie shivering in your sleeping bag while wearing all your clothes. By 2:00 in the afternoon you may be so hot you are wondering how to get more naked without embarrassing yourself. Bring clothes you can layer and unlayer to adapt to changing temperatures.

Always bring warm clothing and rain gear. Weather can change fast here. It's amazing how cold, windy, and downright nasty it can get in June and July, and sometimes even in August. If you are already wet and chilled, the strong afternoon winds in the canyon can make you think you're in the Arctic, not the desert.

Sun, wind, heat, and exercise make you more vulnerable to intoxication than normal. In other words, you get drunker faster in a boat. Reactions become slower, and judgment is clouded. Alcohol is a factor in most drownings on the river, and that last beer can set you and your friends up for a serious dumping. Do yourself and your companions a favor, and quit drinking well before your normal limit. Be aware, too, that the State Police and BLM law enforcement officers strictly enforce DUII laws on the access roads.

Some camping areas have sandy soil that will not hold a tent stake on a windy day. Tie your tent to trees or large rocks.

The Deschutes can be a windy place. The upriver wind that arises most afternoons can make casting difficult, can make your boat feel like the anchor is dragging, and can blow your tent into the river. It's very distracting to be casting into prime steelhead water and suddenly see your tent floating downriver, so stake your tent extremely well. Some sites have sandy soil that will not hold a tent stake. In these places, tie your tent to rocks or trees. Don't underestimate the power of the Deschutes wind, especially if a weather front is moving through. One time I tied my tent to four rocks the size of watermelons. The wind still pushed it around, dragging the four rocks behind it.

Fires

The Deschutes River canyon is dry country, and it doesn't take much to start a roaring grass fire here in summer. Enforcement of fire rules is a top priority with the Oregon State Police and BLM law enforcement officers during the dry season. There is a stiff fine of $500 for violators.

Today, most river users are sensitive to the fire danger. This means that anyone who starts a fire in the dry season will have dozens of people appear out of nowhere and tell him—loudly, unkindly, and maybe accurately—that he is the biggest fool they have ever seen. It also means that if you accidentally start a fire, someone will know about it. Offenders *will* be caught. When caught, they will be held financially responsible for all damages, as well as suppression costs. A few years ago, an unfortunate camper started a grass fire that burned a lot of acres and a few cows. He was spotted by several people, prosecution was started, and he reportedly settled out of court for a dollar amount that was well into six figures.

Extreme Fire Season is from June 1 to October 15. During this period, the fire regulations are:

No open fires or charcoal briquettes except in totally enclosed structures such as a house or RV.

Cook only with commercially manufactured LP (propane, butane) or white gas stoves.

Use only commercially manufactured LP, white gas, or battery lanterns. No candles.

No smoking except in a totally enclosed structure or on-road vehicle, or in a boat that is on the water. Always dispose of the butt in an ashtray or garbage bag. Don't throw it into the bushes or into the water.

The rest of the year, fires may be built only in fire pans—solid metal containers with sides at least two inches high. Fire pans can be purchased commercially, or you can use items such as steel baking pans, oil

During the summer and early fall, the canyon area is tinder dry. Extreme precaution is needed to prevent range fires.

drain pans, or part of a steel drum. Soil is a living organism, and fire pans reduce sterilization of soil as well as contain ashes.

If you are planning a campfire, bring your own wood. It is illegal to cut or burn any wood—dead, live, down, or otherwise—in the river corridor. Even dead trees perform an ecologically useful role. They provide homes for birds and small mammals, and are used for hunting perches, preening and singing, communications (by woodpeckers), food storage, protection from weather, resting, and roosting. They are also an important food source for insect-eating birds.

When done with your fire, don't forget to pack out the ashes when they are cold. If left behind, ashes often end up in the river and cause blackened beaches.

Lanterns and stoves with built-in ignition are preferred because you don't have to dispose of a match.

Water

Drinking water is available only at Maupin City Park, Beavertail, Macks Canyon, and Deschutes River State Park. For all other locations, including boat-in sites, you need to pack your own water or purify river water. Do not drink river water or wash dishes in it unless you purify it by filtration, by chemical treatment, or by boiling more than five minutes.

Because of the hot, arid, windy climate, you will need more liquids than you may be used to (remember Operation Desert Storm?). Therefore, always take more drinking water than you think you'll need. Few things are more discouraging than to be down in the canyon with trout rising all around you, and you need to leave because you are parched and out of water.

There are few places to get water in the canyon, so bring your own. Always bring more than you think you'll need.

Garbage

The preceding four sections dealt with the four elements of matter as defined by the ancient Greek philosophers: earth, air, fire, and water. This section deals with that ubiquitous element of the modern world—garbage.

All drive-in sites have garbage cans. Put all refuse in the can, and make sure the lid is closed tight so garbage-seeking critters can't get in. Often you will find litter around the can. Pick it up and put it in the can before the canyon wind scatters it. Putting a rock on the lid will help keep the lid from blowing off.

Except for North Junction, boat-in sites have no garbage cans. For boaters, the rule about garbage is simple: take it out. Put a plastic trash bag in your boat or raft, and take it with you into camp. At night, close up your garbage bag tightly, and put it in a solid, closed container. Flimsy plastic garbage bags will not deter nocturnal critters such as raccoons and skunks. When you climb out of your tent for a 3 AM call of nature, do you really want to blunder into a skunk?

Don't try to bury or burn anything. Prepare meals in advance or plan them so as to minimize waste. Pack out all grease and leftovers. Don't leave anything behind, including monofilament fishing line, bottle caps, pull tabs, plastic beverage rings, jars, and other notorious booby traps for fish and wildlife. Every year animals die along the Deschutes because of trash left behind by campers. Birds become caught in fishing line and beverage rings . . . and starve. Deer eat metal bottle caps . . . and have their digestive system destroyed. Fish swallow cigarette butts . . . and choke to death. Dispose of these hazards in a manner that is safe for fish and wildlife.

Litter can take an amazingly long time to decompose. Toilet paper takes two to five months, orange peels half a year, and filter cigarette butts 10-12 years. Dispose of all trash, and keep the canyon looking natural.

If you keep any fish (see the regulations in Chapter 7 for what may

be kept) and clean them, don't bury the guts and heads (animals dig them up), or throw them in the river (unpunctured bladders cause them to float and wash up on shore). Put them in your trash bag.

Do not put any trash in the outhouse pits. The rule is, if it isn't toilet paper or didn't come from your body, don't put it in the outhouse pit! As BLM says with great understatement, trash "is very difficult to remove from outhouse pits." There used to be an outhouse at Whitehorse Rapids. It was removed because people kept dumping trash into it, and it could no longer be economically maintained.

Always carry a plastic garbage bag when you drift the river.

Personal Hygiene

BLM advises that you urinate in the river, but frankly I have a hard time recommending this for aesthetic reasons. Imagine drifting around a bend in the river and finding some guy making a golden arch into the water you intend to fish.

You can follow BLM's advice (in an inoffensive and private manner), or, if an outhouse isn't nearby, go in the bushes at least 50 feet from the river and well outside camping areas. This practice will help reduce offensive odors in heavily-used campsites.

As for number two, use the outhouse. In fact, it is illegal to "improperly" dispose of human waste (such as leave it in the bushes). That's right, the state can issue you an "illegal pooping" ticket. Do you really want to be in the bushes with your pants around your ankles, and have some guy in a "bear" hat come after you and write up a ticket? Do you really want to put up with all the bad jokes your so-called friends will make for years afterwards?

You will probably encounter fewer critters in an outhouse then in the bushes. However, since being locked in a small room with something slithery and venomous can disturb an otherwise contemplative act, you should make a quick check to see if a snake has come into the outhouse. Then lift the ring and make sure there are no black widow spiders around the edge. When done with the outhouse, put the lid down. This helps to reduce both odor and flies.

There is no excuse for finding human waste and soiled toilet tissue within 100 yards of an outhouse—yet this is the case too often. It takes less than two minutes to walk 100 yards, even with your legs crossed. Anyone who can't hold on for two minutes should be wearing diapers.

When you arrive at a boat-in or drive-in campsite that has an outhouse, spot its location so you can find your way in the dark, if necessary. Perhaps it's the constant sound of running water, but people seem to get up in the night more when camped on a river. Keep a flashlight and shoes handy when you bed down, know the way to the privy, and use it.

Sometimes, however, you just gotta go and there's no outhouse in sight. In this case, pick a place well outside camping areas and at least 50 feet from the river. Dig a hole six to eight inches deep with a stick, rock, tent stake, or, if you were clever enough to plan ahead, a trowel or shovel. The diameter of the hole depends on your aim. Go in the hole.

Put the tissue in the hole (or pack it out, using a zip-lock bag), then cover the hole with six inches of dirt and make the ground surface appear as natural as possible. Do not, under any circumstances, try to burn the tissue! Incidentally, burying waste too deep actually inhibits decomposition. Six to eight inches is the right depth.

Poor hygiene habits detract greatly from many of the campsites, especially on the lower 24 miles of the river. By the end of the season, some of the flats look like the campers believed toilet tissue was a party decoration—a kind of streamer, perhaps—and the campsite is decorated for a Fete de Feces, or maybe Cinco de Mairdo. Plan ahead. If you are

going to stay on your favorite camp water, and there is no outhouse, bring a trowel so you can bury your waste. Better yet, bring a portable toilet. You can dispose of waste in an outhouse when you reach one.

Feminine hygiene? Keep a zip-lock bag handy to carry out used tissue and other paraphernalia. Then dispose of the contents (but not the plastic bag) in an outhouse when you come to one, or dump the whole thing in a garbage can.

Don't bathe or wash your hair in the river. The soap can take a long time to break down. So does toothpaste, for that matter.

It's true: the Oregon State Police can issue "illegal pooping" tickets. Use the outhouse for #2.

Clean Up after Cooking

Proper cleaning of pots, pans, and other cooking and eating utensils aids greatly in retaining the quality of campsites. Never dump leftovers in the bushes, as it will attract nuisance animals. Put leftovers in a garbage can or in your trash bag.

Consider a soapless cleanup, as described below.

First, scrape leftovers into your plastic trash bag.

Then wipe all cooking and eating utensils with a paper towel to remove excess food. Put the used towels in your trash bag.

Next, scrub utensils with hot water. Dump the water in a waste water sump (available at many drive-in sites), or scoop a small depression in the dirt and strain your wash water through it. Many campers carry a small screen, such as a piece of window screen, and use that to strain wash water. After the water has drained, scrape off the excess food and put it in your trash bag.

Finally, rinse all utensils with boiling water and dispose of the rinse water in the waste water hole. Cover the hole back up with dirt.

You can use a small piece of screen to strain leftovers from wash water.

Floating the River

Boater's Pass. Every person on the Deschutes River in a water craft of any kind is required to have a Boater's Pass. The current fine for not having a Boater's Pass is $53.00 *per person.*

Individual passes may be purchased for daily or seasonal use. If you lose your pass, you may get a duplicate from the place you bought the original. Also, if you purchase a daily pass and cannot go on the scheduled day, you can get a "rain check." To do this, take your permit into any place that sells them—before the date-of-use on the pass—and get a new pass.

You may get a Boater's Pass for a group; the group leader purchases

a single pass for a specific number of unnamed individuals.

At this time, there is no program to limit the number of boats on a section of the river on any particular day. However, such a program may be started sometime after 1995.

Regardless of what kind of water craft you use, you are required to carry a Boater's Pass. (Randy Stetzer photo)

The Boater's Pass program is administered by the State Parks Department. Money from the sale of passes is used to maintain campsites and launching/landing sites on State land, to improve fish and wildlife habitat, and for State law enforcement on the river. A percentage of Boater's Pass money is turned over to BLM, who is a major land owner on the river.

Boater's Passes are available at most tourist-oriented businesses in Maupin, as well as at major metropolitan fishing and sport stores.

Boating Regulations and Guidelines. Some other boating regulations and guidelines are:

You may not operate a motorized watercraft while under the influence of intoxicating liquor or a controlled substance. For a 180-pound person, a six-pack of beer consumed over a four hour period can put you legally "under the influence." However, "stressors" like exercise, wind, and sun, can cause a person to act or feel intoxicated with less alcohol.

Everyone in a boat, raft, or other watercraft must have an approved personal flotation device (PFD; for example, a life jacket). It is a fact that 85% of people who drown in boating accidents would have lived if they had been wearing a PFD. In the last five years, 110 people have died in boating accidents in Oregon. Only 11 were wearing a PFD.

Between the northern boundary of the Warm Springs Reservation (near river mile 69) and Buckhollow Creek (below Sherars Falls) motors are not permitted from May 15 to October 15. After October 15, motorboats are allowed in this area if they have a self-issuing permit.

Between Buckhollow Creek and Macks Canyon Campground motors are prohibited between June 15 and September 30.

From Macks Canyon Campground to Heritage Landing, motorboats are excluded on alternating weekends between June 15 and September 30.

Motorboats are limited to a maximum of seven passengers, and no more than two round trips a day.

Between Moody Rapids and Rattlesnake Rapids, motorboats may not stop except for an emergency.

All but the first two of these regulations were adopted in early 1993 and will be reviewed in 1994.

Streamflow. You can find out the discharge from Pelton Dam by calling the Portland General Electric fishline. The number is 1-800-632-3474 (632-FISH). This report is updated daily. Normal summer flows are around 4,000 cubic feet per second, or less. Anything over 5,000 cfs is considered high volume and indicates poor fishing.

Flora and Fauna to Avoid

Poison Ivy. Some people call this poison oak, although poison oak has a leaf shaped like an oak leaf, and what grows along the Deschutes has a leaf shaped like an ivy leaf. Actually, neither is an oak nor an ivy. They are sumacs. Regardless, some areas along the river abound in poison ivy. It grows primarily in bankside areas near the water. Contact with bare skin can cause an uncomfortable rash for most people.

If some of the oil from the plant's leaves gets on your clothing, rod grip, or family dog, it may then be transferred onto your skin. From there you may rub it over major portions of your body. The best way to avoid problems with poison ivy is to avoid the plant completely. See the section in Chapter 7 on wading wet for advice to fishermen who insist on wearing shorts in the canyon.

There is a product on the market that does a good job of removing the rash-causing oil before it becomes a big problem. The product has the trade name of Tecnu and is available in many outdoor stores. I always carries a tube of it in my fishing bag when I go to the Deschutes.

Rattlesnakes. There are rattlesnakes in the Deschutes canyon, as well as many kinds of non-venomous snakes. Rattlesnakes are part of the desert ecology of the Deschutes canyon, so don't kill a rattlesnake if you find one. It does no particular good to do so, and much harm. While you needn't be frightened of them, you should be careful and respectful. With a few wise precautions you should have no snake problems on the Deschutes, and could fish for years without seeing one.

The type of rattlesnake found on the Deschutes is the Western Rattlesnake (Crotalus viridis). They come in a variety of colors and habitat preferences, but are the same species of snake. Mature snakes are seldom longer than 30 inches and have a wide triangular head.

These snakes live in dens in rock piles, primarily on south-facing slopes lacking trees and other vegetation. They hunt small mammals, such as mice, near their dens. During hot weather they are active primarily at night, but during cooler weather they will hunt in the daytime. When it starts to freeze at night—around late September—they hibernate and don't emerge again until almost seven months later. For some people, this seems like a good reason to go fishing in the winter.

Rattlesnakes want to avoid people even more than people want to avoid them. So give them a chance to get away. If you stay on beaten trails, you are more likely to see a snake in time to avoid a collision, but if you wander through the brush you may surprise a rattlesnake. Rattlesnakes don't like surprises.

Snakes are very sensitive to vibration, so if they can feel you coming they have a chance to hide. I often carry a wading staff on dry land and thump it on the ground as I walk. I do this in the belief that the snakes will sense my approach and get the heck out of the way. The same approach can work on rock piles. Go slow enough for snakes to hear you coming, and give them the right of way.

Don't put your hands or your feet in places you can't see. When wading the river, look at that clump of streamside grass before you put your hand on it; there might be a snake cooling off on it.

Everywhere you go, keep an ear out, as well as an eye. A threatened snake will often (but not always) rattle. The sound is more like a buzz than the rocks-in-a-can sound common to Hollywood westerns. The buzz is a warning: get out of my face. The snake wants to get away from you, so back away slowly and give it a chance. You'll both be happier.

If you encounter a dead snake, treat it with respect. Even dead snakes are dangerous and can inject venom. Don't let children handle them under any circumstances. If you have a dog, don't let it run through the brush since it may surprise a snake and get bitten.

Other Critters. There are some very small scorpions in the canyon, although in the last ten years I have never seen one (though I haven't looked real hard, either). They are not especially dangerous, but it might be a good idea to shake out boots and other clothing in the morning.

There are a few black widow spiders, as well. They are very shy and are fond of dark places. For this reason they are occasionally found in outhouse stools. Lift the ring before you sit down, and make a quick check. Doubtless you will find nothing, but . . .

3

Pelton Dam to Trout Creek

This section of the river is very popular because it offers excellent trout fishing, easy boating, and access to 16.5 miles of river bank, including six miles on the Warm Springs Reservation. River drifters will encounter no rapids more difficult than Class I.

Public facilities adjacent to the river include four places you can drive to, two of which have boat ramps; three drive-in camps; and a liberal scattering of quality boat-in camps. At this time, there is no drinking water available in this part of the river, so be sure to bring plenty of your own.

Directions to, and descriptions of, all facilities in this stretch are given below, and are listed by access point. See the road map and the river maps for an overview of this area. In this chapter, "Pelton Dam" is used in a generic sense. There are two Pelton Dams, and the lower one (from which the Lower Deschutes begins) is properly called Pelton Reregulation Dam.

Warm Springs Boat Ramp

Public facilities near the community of Warm Springs include a boat ramp, and highway pull-outs on the east bank of a short segment of the river.

Getting There. US 26 crosses the Deschutes at Warm Springs near mile post 105. This is about 15 miles northwest of Madras, and 50 miles southeast of Government Camp. The turn-off for the boat ramp is a quarter mile south of the bridge, just across from the Rainbow Market (where snacks, fishing licenses, and Boaters' Passes may be purchased).

Facilities. There is a good gravel boat ramp here. Rafts can be assembled and launched at several places near the ramp, but do not assemble rafts on the ramp itself. Parking is ample, and there is a double outhouse and garbage cans. Camping is not permitted here, but both Mecca Flat and Dry Creek (see below) are nearby.

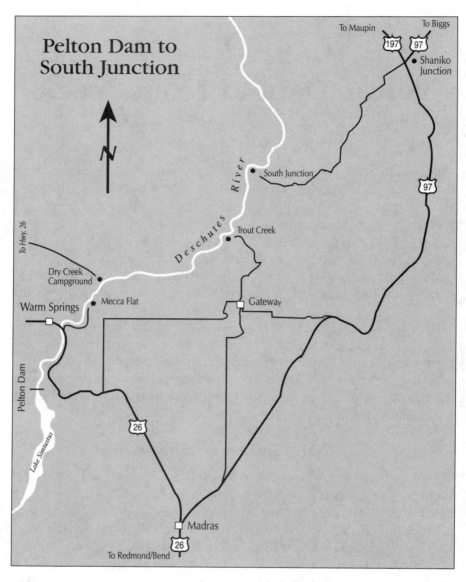

Pelton Dam to South Junction

To Maupin
To Biggs
197 97
Shaniko Junction

97

South Junction

Deschutes River

Trout Creek

To Hwy. 26

Dry Creek Campground

Warm Springs • Mecca Flat

Gateway

Pelton Dam

Lake Simtustus

26

26
Madras

To Redmond/Bend

River Access. There is public access to the east bank of the river along US 26 from the bridge to a point about one mile upstream. Beyond that is private property. The bank is low in this section, and river access is easy. There are several good pull-outs along US 26 where you can park your car. I think everyone should fish this section of the river at least once. Here you can cast your fly amid discarded fast-food

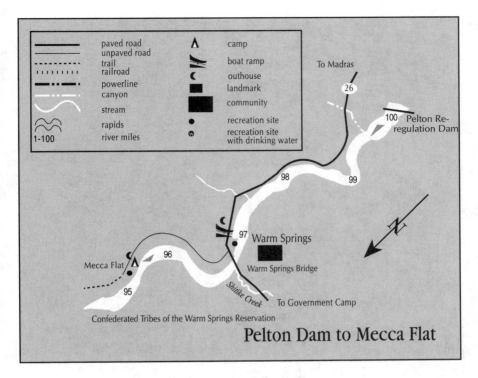

Legend

paved road	
unpaved road	
trail	
railroad	
powerline	
canyon	
stream	
rapids	
1-100	river miles

Λ	camp
boat ramp	
outhouse	
landmark	
community	
•	recreation site
⊛	recreation site with drinking water

To Madras

26

100 Pelton Re-regulation Dam

98   99

97 Warm Springs

Mecca Flat 96

Warm Springs Bridge

95

Shitike Creek

To Government Camp

Confederated Tribes of the Warm Springs Reservation

Pelton Dam to Mecca Flat

cartons, empty bottles and cans, and the noise of high-speed traffic. Thus primed, you'll be ready to appreciate what the rest of the canyon has to offer.

The west bank of the river here is part of Confederated Tribes of Warm Springs (CTWS) and is off-limits to non-tribal members.

Mecca Flat

Mecca provides access to 7.5 miles of river bank, but its amenities as a camp are slim. Facilities are limited to two outhouses; however there is no overnight camping fee.

Getting There. From the east end of the bridge at Warm Springs, turn north onto a dirt road between the Rainbow Rafting/gas station and the Deschutes Trailer Court. Three roads fork off this dirt road. The first road goes to the trailer court, the second is a private driveway. Take the third road (left turn); there is no sign for this road. Proceed 1.5 miles to the Mecca Flat parking area. The road to Mecca is dirt and has some large potholes in it. It can be negotiated by most cars, but if your vehicle is low-slung you might want to avoid this road. RVs and cars pulling trail-

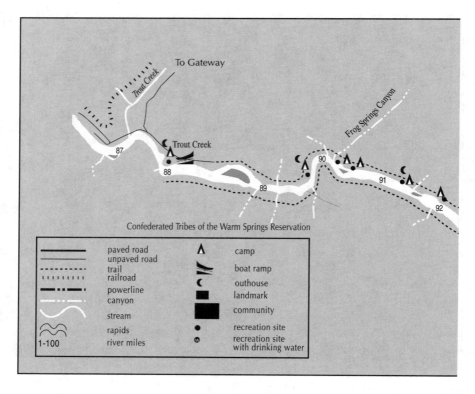

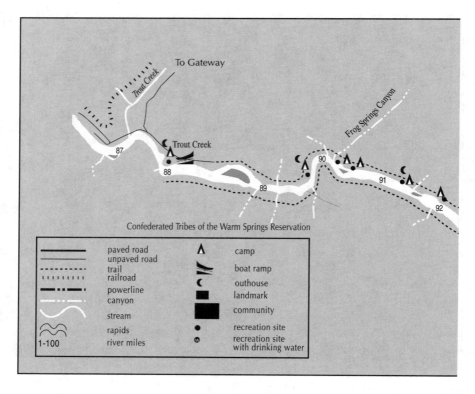

——————	paved road	Λ	camp
	unpaved road		
- - - - - - -	trail	⤚	boat ramp
׀׀׀׀׀׀׀׀	railroad	C	outhouse
—··—··—	powerline	▪	landmark
	canyon		
〜〜	stream	▬	community
〜〜	rapids	●	recreation site
1-100	river miles	ⓦ	recreation site with drinking water

ers may have trouble. This road can become impassable after a heavy rain, and even four-wheel drive vehicles can have difficulty getting up the hill.

Camping and Facilities. The camping areas are heavily used and show it. Little vegetation remains, so avoid driving on the few plants that are left. Camp at the dirt/grass flat south of the parking area, or use one of the two tent sites near the river about a quarter mile south of the parking area. An outhouse is located 200 yards upstream from the parking area, and another is about one-half mile downstream.

River Access. There is access to almost one mile of river upstream from the Mecca Flat parking area. For downstream access, cross the stile over the barbed wire fence adjacent to the parking area. Downstream from this point you can get to 7.5 miles of river bank, as far as the Trout Creek campground. There is a trail along the river, so little bank-climbing is required.

If you need to cover distance quickly or have a mountain bike, use the dirt road farther up the bank. To reach this road from the parking

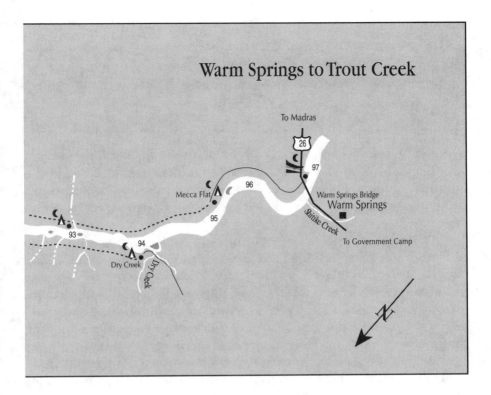

Warm Springs to Trout Creek

area, cross over the stile, then go about 100 feet to your right. This road (closed to motor vehicles) runs all the way to Trout Creek. Watch for snakes; they sometimes sun on the road.

There is now a horse gate at Mecca Flat, so riders have access to the road. However, the road crosses private property about one mile downstream, and horses may not pass through at this time.

Dry Creek

Dry Creek is the only non-tribal access to the Deschutes within the Warm Springs Reservation. You may camp only at Dry Creek, and you may fish for trout or steelhead along six miles of river bank downstream from the campground. A special permit is required to fish or camp here. Permits may be purchased by the day or for the year; see Chapter 7 for more details on Warm Springs Permits.

Getting There. On US 26, just north of the Deschutes River bridge at Warm Springs, there is a large sign for the paved road to Kah-nee-ta Resort. Take this road (Warm Springs Route 3) north for 3.1 miles, to

> *"We did not inherit this land and its resources from our ancestors: we are only borrowing it from our children's children and their children."* From the Constitution of the Confederated Tribes of Warms Springs.

where you see the sign for Dry Creek on the right. Turn right onto a broad, gravel road. The road soon splits; take the right fork and go 1.6 miles to another fork in the road. The right fork leads to a large, modern water treatment plant. Take the left fork and go 0.2 miles to the campground.

Camping and Facilities. This is the only public campground on the Warm Springs Reservation. Although level ground is at a premium, there are five or six primitive campsites. Some of these are reached by very rough roads, so drive carefully. A Warm Springs permit is required to camp here. Facilities are a conveniently located high-tech outhouse, garbage cans near the outhouse, and four tables. There is no drinking water. Boat or raft launching is not permitted here.

River Access. Just downstream from the outhouse there is a dirt road with a locked gate across it. From this gate to a point about six miles downstream (opposite the Trout Creek Campground) there is good

If you have a Warm Springs Permit you may fish six miles of river bank between this locked gate at Dry Creek and a point opposite the Trout Creek campground. You may walk or use a bicycle.

bank access from the dirt road. You may walk or use a bicycle. The road is 10 to 15 feet above the river in most places, so some bank-climbing is needed to get to the fishing.

Trout Creek

One of the larger and more developed campgrounds on the river, Trout Creek is also the jumping-off point to 7.5 miles of upstream river bank. It is an easy day's drift from Warm Springs and is the only reasonable take-out point before Whitehorse Rapids; once you drift past here, you are committed to the next 29 miles of river.

Getting There. To reach the Trout Creek campground, you must first get to the community of Gateway. There are three main routes to Gateway, depending on where you start, as described below.

Getting to Gateway From Warm Springs. From the Deschutes River bridge at Warm Springs, go southeast 5.3 miles on US 26 to the top of the canyon rim. Make a hairpin left turn (careful!), then turn right in about 200 yards (the road you turned onto is NW Deschutes Drive, but there is no sign stating the fact for another mile). Go 3.0 miles and make a sharp right turn onto NW Juniper Lane. After another 4.4 miles, the road takes a 90-degree right turn, then a hairpin left, and winds downhill 1.8 miles to the little community of Gateway (no services). Go slowly through Gateway. Turn left just before the old train station. There is a road sign here pointing to "Deschutes Rv Trout Cr."

Getting to Gateway From Madras. From the US 26/US 97 junction, go north on US 97 2.4 miles. Turn left where there is a road sign for "Gateway" (in 0.75 mile this road becomes Clark Drive). You come to a "Y" 3.9 miles after the turn-off from US 97. Take the left fork (straight ahead). The road makes a sharp right 2.0 miles from the "Y" and becomes Bulkey Lane. In another 2.0 miles—after several sharp turns—you will reach the community of Gateway (no services). Go slowly through Gateway. Turn right just past the railroad tracks. There is a road sign here pointing to "Deschutes Rv Trout Cr."

Getting to Gateway From Maupin. Coming south on US 97, turn right at milepost 81, about 35 miles from Maupin. There is a sign for "Richardson's Recreational Ranch" opposite the turn-off, but there is no sign for Trout Creek. After 2.9 miles, turn right onto Emerson Drive. There is a sign for "BLM Trout Cr/Recreation Site." Proceed 3.0 miles to where the road comes to a "T." Turn right, and proceed into Gateway (no services). These last miles before Gateway are on gravel road. Go slowly through Gateway. Turn right just past the railroad tracks. There is a road sign here pointing to "Deschutes Rv Trout Cr."

Getting to Trout Creek from Gateway. Once you have made the turn onto the Trout Creek road at Gateway, go 4.2 miles down this road to where it T's. At the T, go left (there is a sign). The road soon turns right and comes to another T. Turn left for the main campground and boat ramp; there is a loop with campsites to the right.

Most of the roads to Gateway are paved, but soon after you make the turn to Trout Creek, the road becomes gravel, then dirt with large rocks. It can be extremely rough, depending on when it was last graded. Most cars should have no problems with this portion of the road as long as they go slowly, however some RVs may have trouble coming out because of a steep graveled hill.

Camping and Facilities. Trout Creek has a good gravel boat ramp near the campground entrance, plenty of parking suitable for boat trailers, and many level designated sites for tents, trailers, and RVs. Most sites have a table. There are some tent sites along the river near the boat ramp; these are most suited to boaters stopping here overnight. Camping fee is $3 per night. A fee station is located at the campground entrance.

Amenities include a large double outhouse near the boat ramp, two singles at the south end, and two more on a loop at the north end. There

are garbage cans near the boat ramp and at several other locations, and a waste water sump at the south end. A 1993 addition was a recycling center for aluminum and glass, so separate your trash. A campground host resides here in summer. There is no drinking water at Trout Creek, although there are plans to add it sometime in the future.

River Access. Bank access downstream from Trout Creek is difficult due to private prop-

There are many good trails along the river between Trout Creek and Mecca Flat.

erty, but upstream travel is easy all the way to Mecca Flat, about 7.5 miles. Your travel options throughout this stretch are varied. Streamside foot trails are numerous. Or, if you want to make time, you may travel by foot or mountain bike along the dirt road above the river (closed to motor vehicles; and watch for snakes, as they sometimes sun themselves on this road). Hikers and walk-in anglers will find parking at the south end near the trails.

In addition to foot and bike traffic, BLM permits horse travel on this road; the gate is just before the entrance to the campground. To get to this point you will have to trailer your horse down from Gateway, which may be hard on both horse and trailer, depending on the current state of the road bed. Horse access along the river road is a round trip deal: it ends at private property about 5.5 miles upstream. At this time, the private landowner does not allow horses across his property.

Boat-in Campsites

River miles (RM) are measured from the confluence with the Columbia. Drift miles (DM) are measured from the boat ramp at Warm Springs. By convention, "West" refers to the left bank when facing downstream; "East" refers to the right bank when facing downstream. See Chapter 2 for further discussion of boat-in camping.

DM 4.1/RM 92.8 (East) A fence with concrete posts and tubular metal rails comes down to the river. A small campsite for one or two tents is just downstream from the fence. An outhouse is up the bank on the access road.

DM 4.9/RM 92.0 (East) There is an island on the Reservation side of the river. A short distance downstream from this island there is a grassy flat on the right which offers good camping. Some sites near the river have shade. This is a large area where a number of people can camp, but there is no outhouse. There is a long shallow area of quiet water for landing boats.

DM 5.5/RM 91.4 (East) Just past a large island on the right side, there is a flat with excellent camping. It has numerous campsites, some with shade, and there is an outhouse. There are several good boat landing places.

DM 6.5/RM 90.4 (East) Several alder snags are sticking up from the water near the bank. There is a lava cliff behind the camp, with a large

Shade trees have been planted in several boat-in campsites. They often have a bucket so campers can water them.

pile of lava rocks at its base. Several tent sites exist here, some with good shade but most without. There is no outhouse.

DM 6.8/RM 90.1 (East) Just below a tight group of islands, you can see a canyon descending to the river on the right side. A wooden bridge crosses the creek that runs through the canyon. There are two or three pleasant shady tent sites, but no outhouse. This area is called Frog Springs.

DM 7.3/RM 89.6 (East) As the river starts to turn right, there is a large pile of lava rocks on the east side. There is space for two or three tents. An outhouse is located here.

DM 8.9/RM 88 (East) Below Big Island, the river makes a gradual bend to the left. Trout Creek campground appears on the flat on the right. The boat ramp is around a sharp right bend. Trout Creek has a low bank, and several tent sites near the river are suitable for boat-in use (see above).

4

Trout Creek to Maupin Area

This section of river is similar to the section above it, except the boating is more difficult. This makes it a popular drift for whitewater enthusiasts, who test their skills in rapids like the Four Chutes, Buckskin Mary, and the notorious Class IV three-mile long Whitehorse Rapids. Fishing for trout and steelhead can be excellent throughout this part of the river.

Trout Creek, the south end of this section, is described in Chapter 3. Maupin, the north end, is described in Chapter 5. Other than these two end points, South Junction is the only drive-in access to this part of the river, and it is described below.

Boats and rafts cannot be easily taken out at South Junction, so once you start drifting from Trout Creek you are committed to the next 29 miles of river. Therefore, boaters need to be skilled and properly prepared.

Boat-in campsites on this stretch are described following the section on South Junction.

South Junction

South Junction is a pleasant campground, offering good fishing on about 1.5 miles of public river bank sandwiched between private property.

Getting There. See the road map in Chapter 3. The turn-off to South Junction is where highways US 197 and US 97 come together, about 22 miles southeast of the Maupin bridge, and 33 miles north of the US 26/US 97 junction in Madras. At the US 97/US 197 junction, take the gravel road to the west; there is a sign for "South Junction." After 7.4 miles, the road drops down the canyon to the river. The final stretch has numerous curves and no guard rail. Be careful, and don't be too eager to reach the fishing; gravel is slippery stuff. The road splits 9.1 miles from the 97/197 junction. Take the right fork, and proceed 0.5 mile into the campground.

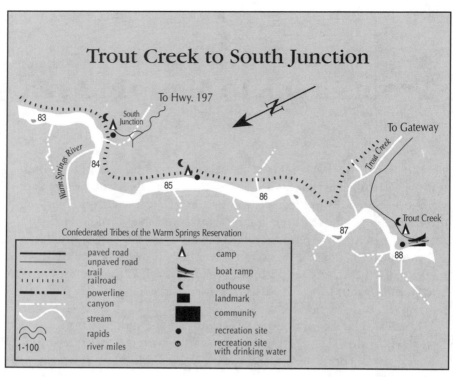

Trout Creek to South Junction

To Hwy. 197

South Junction

To Gateway

Warm Springs River

Trout Creek

Trout Creek

83
84
85
86
87
88

Confederated Tribes of the Warm Springs Reservation

paved road	⋀	camp
unpaved road		boat ramp
trail		
railroad	☾	outhouse
powerline	■	landmark
canyon		
stream	▬	community
rapids	●	recreation site
1-100 river miles	ⓦ	recreation site with drinking water

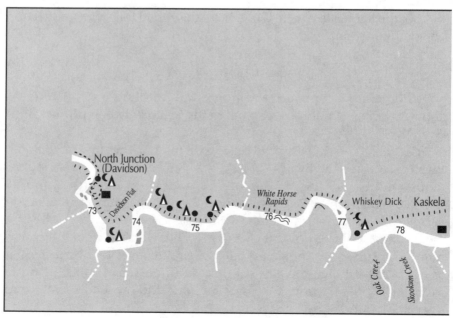

North Junction
(Davidson)

Davidson Flat

White Horse Rapids

Whiskey Dick   Kaskela

73
74
75
76
77
78

Oak Creek

Skookum Creek

The camping area ends at the second (north-most) outhouse, but the road continues another 0.4 mile, then ends at a gate and turnaround. There is no camping down here, no place to park, and no reason to be here unless you are an owner of one of the ranches beyond the gate.

Camping and Facilities. South Junction is a semi-developed campground perched high above the river. It has a handful of established campsites, most of which offer a table and a juniper tree for shade. The camping fee is $3 per night. There is a fee station as you enter the campground.

Facilities include two outhouses, one at each end of the campground; garbage cans near the outhouses; and two waste water sumps, one at the southern outhouse and another in the middle of the campground.

Launching a raft at South Junction is possible, though it is hard work. The launching site is opposite the north-most outhouse; look for an aluminum gate near the stile over the barbed-wire fence. Drag your raft through this gate (be sure to close it behind you!) and across the railroad tracks. Then drag it down the steep hill, and carry it over the steps that lead into the river. It is an arduous process, and saves a 40-60 minute float from Trout Creek. Is it worth it?

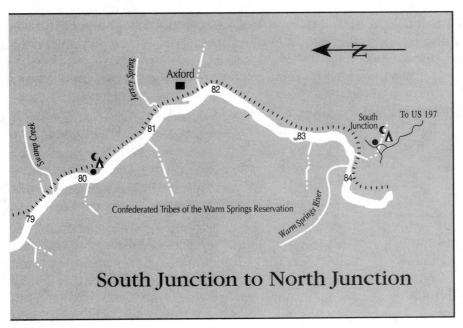

South Junction to North Junction

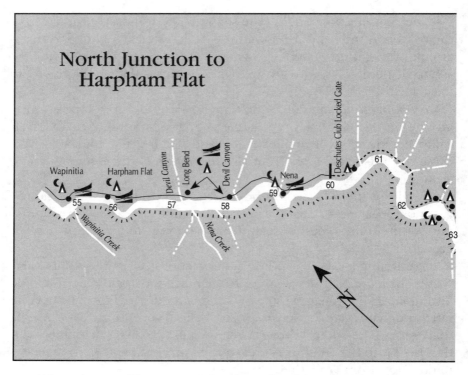

North Junction to Harpham Flat

River Access. There are 1.5 miles of public river bank at South Junction. The campground is about 50 feet above the river, and in some places you have to do a bit of clambering up and down the banks to get to the fishing.

The campground is bordered on the south by private property, so river access is limited in this direction. Some people walk up the railroad tracks until they reach public land above Green Valley Farms. See Chapter 2 for information about walking on the railroad tracks.

To the north, you soon run into private property which extends a couple of miles down the river before public land is reached again.

Boat-in Campsites

River miles (RM) are measured from the confluence with the Columbia. Drift miles (DM) are measured from the boat ramp at Warm Springs. By convention, "West" refers to the left bank when facing downstream; "East" refers to the right bank when facing downstream. See Chapter 2 for further discussion of boat-in camping.

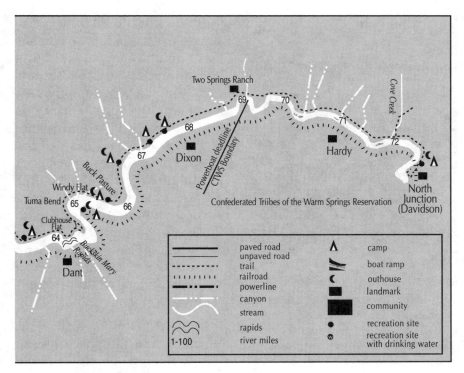

DM 11.6/RM 85.3 (East) About one mile below Trout Creek Rapids, you drift past two islands. The first is on the right, the second about a quarter mile further and on the left. Just past this latter island, a flat opens up on the right. Look for a point that forms a riffle. The camping area begins at this point and continues downstream more than a quarter mile. There are numerous tent sites, many with shade. The outhouse is in the upper third of the camping area, about 250 feet from the river.

DM 13.4/RM 83.5 (East) The Warm Springs River enters on the left, and you soon pass through a small rapids on a right bend. The South Junction drive-in camp is on your right. Because the bank is steep and the campsites and facilities are well above the river, this is not a convenient boat-in camp. However, there are a few small tent sites scattered along the riverbank.

DM 16.9/RM 80.0 (East) After you drift past the buildings at Axford, the river makes a left turn. Downstream from this point, the "Posted" signs are no longer seen, and you are into public land again. However, it is almost one mile—down a stretch of straight, flat water—before there is

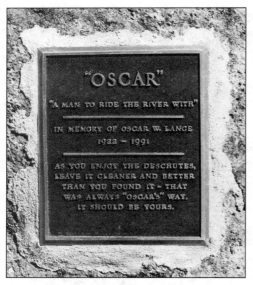

At Whiskey Dick campsite, a memorial has been erected to the late Oscar Lange, long time river guide and former owner of Oscar's Sporting Goods in Madras.

enough flat land for a campground. Look for the remains of an old wing dam angling upstream, with a small rapids below it. A large camping area begins just above the rapids and extends downstream about a quarter mile. Some sites have shade, especially at the upstream end. The outhouse is up the bank at the point where the rapids end. This whole area is the mother lode of poison ivy. The bank abounds in it, and plants can be found more than 50 feet from the river.

DM 19.5/RM 77.4 (East) A mile and a half past Kaskela, the river makes a 90-degree right turn as it heads into the Mutton Mountains. At this turn, there is a large flat on the right bank with many pleasant campsites. There are two outhouses here. This is the last large campsite before Whitehorse Rapids, which is about a mile and a half ahead.

This area is called Whiskey Dick, although Whiskey Dick proper is across the river.

There are several one-tent campsites along Whitehorse Rapids. None has an outhouse.

DM 21.7/RM 75.2 (East) Near the end of Whitehorse Rapids, the river bends to the right and continues straight for about one-half mile. As you drift around the bend that begins this straight stretch, you can see an outhouse on the right. This is the beginning of a long, sometimes rocky camping area that extends downriver almost three-quarters of a mile to the next two camps. Good sites are scattered throughout. Some have shade.

DM 22.0/RM 74.9 (East) About a quarter mile below the site described above there is another outhouse.

DM 22.4/RM 74.5 (East) At the end of the straight stretch described above, the river snakes around a tall basalt wall on the left side, and a large flat appears on the right. This camping area is at the end of Whitehorse Rapids. It can accommodate large numbers of people and has an outhouse. A wooden dispenser of plastic trash bags (free!) can be found in the middle of the flat.

DM 23.4/RM 73.5 (East) The river makes a sharp 90-degree left, then a right, then another 90-degree right; this last turn is flanked on the left by a high wall of columnar basalt. These turns have been around the peninsula of Davidson Flat. The campsite is at the north end and is suited to large groups. There are two outhouses. Notice that the area just south of the campground is private property; it is well fenced.

DM 24.3/RM 72.6 (East) About 200 feet below the railroad bridge at North Junction, there is a campsite in the trees. It is suitable for two or three small-to-medium sized groups. The campsites are mostly shaded, one by a grove of large trees. There is an outhouse at the south end, and several garbage cans as well. Assuming that you are being a good camper and are "packing it out," you are welcome to use the garbage

The railroad bridge at North Junction. The campsite here is the last public camping for 5 miles.

cans here to lighten your load for the rest of the trip.

Starting at North Junction and continuing downstream for the next 13 miles, you will often see signs on the right bank saying, "Private Property/x Miles To Next Campground." These signs are handy indicators of private/public ownership. They are not strictly accurate, however. What they really show is how far it is to the next public land on the right bank. There may be a campground sooner on the left side. Also, when you reach public land again on the right side, there may or may not be a campsite there.

DM 27.9/RM 69.0 (East) Powerboat deadline, fishing deadline, northern boundary of Warm Spring Reservation. This is not a camping area.

After drifting through some large "S" curves, you enter a straight stretch. On the flat on the right you can see private property signs, a metal silo, fences, and other ranch-looking objects. This is Two Springs Ranch. Looking back into the trees, you can see the Powerboat

You will often see signs like this when you drift between North Junction and Maupin.

Deadline sign. Powerboats may not travel upstream beyond this point.

This is also a fishing deadline. The river is closed to all fishing between this point and Pelton Dam from January 1, until the fourth Saturday in April.

This point is also the northern boundary of the Warm Springs Reservation. Downstream from here, some of the land on the west side is open to the public.

DM 29.4/RM 67.5 (East) The long flat of Two Springs Ranch (see above) comes to an end, and the river bends left. About a quarter mile below this bend, look for a railroad signal light on the left bank. Opposite this light there is a

> *"River conditions mirror what happens in the entire water-shed, including what happens on dry land. To take care of the fish, you must take care of the land, especially the area near the river."* Steve Pribyl, fisheries biologist, Oregon Department of Fish and Wildlife.

camping area with an outhouse on the right bank.

DM 29.6/RM 67.3 (East) After the campsite described above, the river splits into two chutes around a barely submerged gravel bar. Just below the right chute there is a camping area. Some sites have trees. There is no outhouse here, but the road is just above the campsite, and you can easily walk a few hundred yards upstream to find an outhouse.

DM 30.2/RM 66.7 (East) Three large transformers can be seen grouped together on the power lines on the right side. About 350 yards downstream, there is a camping area on the right bank. A few small sites are along the river and have shade. The outhouse is across the road, and a few more tent sites can be found near it. About 200 feet downstream there are some more sites in a grassy area. There is no shade there, but the boat landing is better.

DM 31.1/RM 65.8 (East) The river makes a long bend to the right around a large, privately-owned flat known as "Buck Pasture," and begins a half mile straight, flat glide. As you enter the straight section there is a long row of alder trees on the right side, and about 150 yards below them is a small gravel bar near the right bank. Public land and the camping area begin just below this gravel bar.

There are many good tent sites for the next quarter mile. Many sites have shade trees. The outhouse is 200 yards below the start of the public land.

While this is a good camping area, be forewarned that it is known as "Windy Flat," and sometimes with good reason. Make sure your boat and gear are well tied down.

DM 31.7/RM 65.2 (West) The river makes a near 180-degree turn known as "Tuma Bend." In the middle of this turn you can spot an outhouse on the flat on the left. There are many places to camp here, and a few don't have any rocks. There are fewer places to land a boat, however.

DM 33.4/RM 63.5 (East) After Buckskin Mary Rapids, the river drops through three chutes while making a long right turn, then drops through another small chute on the left turn. These are called the "Four Chutes," and there are several campsites in the area.

After Buckskin Mary, about two-thirds of the way to the first chute, there is a campsite with some shade. The outhouse is behind a large tree near the road. This site and the next one are heavily used, and thus devoid of grass. The sandy soil blows around, and camping here on a windy day can be a gritty experience.

DM 33.9/RM 63.0 (East) After the first of the Four Chutes (see above), there is a campsite with an outhouse. See the comments above about wind and sand.

DM 34.1/RM 62.8 (East) After the second chute, there is a campsite, but no outhouse.

DM 34.3/RM 62.6 (East) After the last of the Four Chutes, there is a house on the right with a high concrete bulkhead. Just downstream from this house, but 200 yards upstream from a sign that says "1.1 Miles to Next Campground," there is a small campsite with no outhouse.

DM 34.4/RM 62.5 (West) The river turns left, and a flat opens up on the left. The river bank is high, but soon drops lower as you drift downstream. There is a shallow but adequate place to land a boat. An outhouse can be seen above the boat landing. This is a broad, flat camping area with no shade whatsoever.

DM 36.5/RM 60.4 (East) About 200 yards below a midstream island you can find a small campsite tucked behind alders on the right bank. About 100 yards downstream from the camp you can see a private property sign stating, "1.3 Miles to Next Campground." There is no outhouse.

This is the last camping area before the Locked Gate (DM 36.9/RM 60.0). Beyond this point, the campgrounds are on the right bank and are drive-in sites. They are described in Chapter 5.

5

Maupin Area

This is the most popular section of the river. It offers excellent whitewater boating between Long Bend and Sandy Beach (above Sherars Falls), and summer weekends can take on a carnival atmosphere in this area. In addition, trout fishing can be good, and there are many steelhead runs. This area is also the best place to fish for chinook salmon.

Maupin is the hub of this activity. Although it is a small town (population 460), Maupin's economy is highly—and increasingly—dependent on tourism, and offers many services for those using the Deschutes. See Chapter 10 for a directory of Maupin businesses of interest to recreationists.

From Maupin, a rough gravel access road parallels the river upstream as far as the Locked Gate, beyond which you may travel only on foot. Downstream from Maupin there is a paved road next to the river as far as Sherars Bridge. A rough gravel road continues along the river bank another 17 miles to Macks Canyon campground. It is possible, but not easy, to continue below Macks Canyon on foot.

Oak Springs and Sherars Bridge are two other places besides Maupin that you can drive to on this stretch of the river. The sections below describe how to reach all three drive-in access points, and how to reach the river (by car and by foot) upstream and downstream from Maupin.

There are numerous campgrounds on the river access roads leading from Maupin. These are described

Maupin is in the middle of the most extensive road-access section of the river.

at the end of the chapter. No boat-in sites for the west side are listed since there are so many excellent facilities on the east side of the river.

Getting There

Driving directions and river access in the Maupin area are detailed below.

Getting to Maupin. Maupin is on US 197 where it crosses the Deschutes. From US 26, turn onto SR 216 (between mileposts 71 and 72) and go 27 miles east to the junction with US 197. Turn right onto 197; Maupin is three miles to the south. From Madras, take US 97 33 miles to the 197/97 junction; bear left onto US 197, and go another 22 miles to Maupin. From The Dalles, travel 45 miles south on US 197.

Getting to Oak Springs. The turn-off to Oak Springs is on US 197 between mileposts 40 and 37 (mysteriously, mileposts 38 and 39 are missing), about 3.0 miles north of the junction of US 197 and SR 216 (the part that comes from US 26). There is an ODFW hatchery sign at the turn-off, and warning signs one half mile before. Turn east onto a paved road and proceed 1.9 miles to where the pavement ends. A steep dirt road leads another 1.3 miles to the Oak Springs fish hatchery. Continue past the hatchery until you get to the railroad tracks. Park in the track area, far enough away that your car will not be flattened by a passing freight train. There are no facilities here. From Oak Springs, you may walk upstream or downstream along various foot trails near the river. The river bank is not high in most areas.

Getting to Sherars Bridge. SR 216 connects US 97 at Grass Valley with US 197 at Tygh Valley. It crosses the Deschutes at Sherars Bridge. If you are travelling on either US 97 or US 197, turn onto SR 216 and follow it to Sherars Bridge, about 21 miles west of Grass Valley, and eight miles east of Tygh Valley. The east side access roads (described below) intersect SR 216 at Sherars. If your eyes glazed over while reading the above description, take a look at the road map and the mists of confusion should evaporate.

The Sherars Bridge area is used primarily for bait and salmon fishing. A few anglers park here and walk upstream or downstream on the railroad tracks to get to fishing on the west side of the river; see the comments about the railroad tracks in Chapter 2.

Getting Upriver from Maupin. Turn onto the road that forks off US 197 near the south end of the bridge, just opposite the Oasis Resort. This

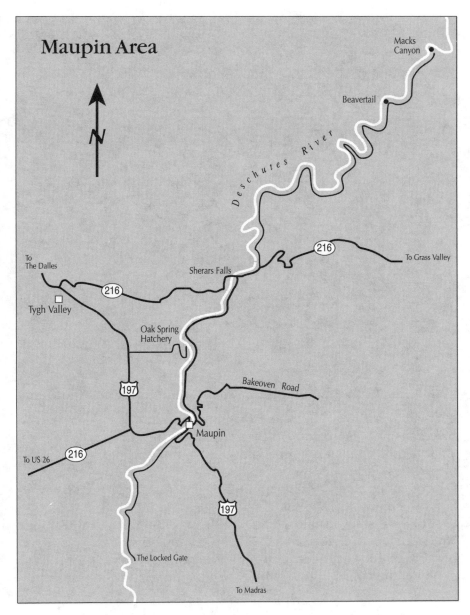

Maupin Area

road goes 6.9 miles upstream to the Locked Gate. It is a broad, but often rough, gravel road until you get to Harpham Flat (3.4 miles), where many people put in or take out their boats and rafts. Beyond Harpham Flat, the road deteriorates. The rocks are bigger, the holes are deeper,

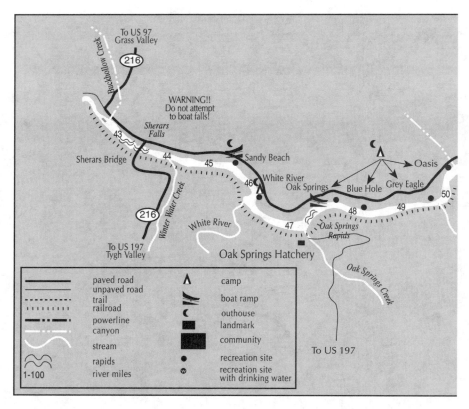

the road is narrower. Just when you think your car will break into more pieces than a Balkan republic, the road ends at the Locked Gate.

The road continues 13 miles beyond the Locked Gate, however it is sometimes on public land, and sometimes on private land. The only form of public access that is permitted on this section of road is foot traffic (no bikes).

For the first seven miles beyond the Locked Gate, public and private land mingle; watch the signs carefully so you know when you are on public land and have access to the river, and when you must stay on the road. For the remaining six miles to North Junction, the east bank is almost all private land.

A couple of miles above the Locked Gate is the Gatekeeper's house. All walk-ins must sign in and out here. The register is outside, near the front door.

Getting Downriver from Maupin to Sherars Bridge. Turn onto Bakeoven Road at the south end of the bridge over the Deschutes. There is a

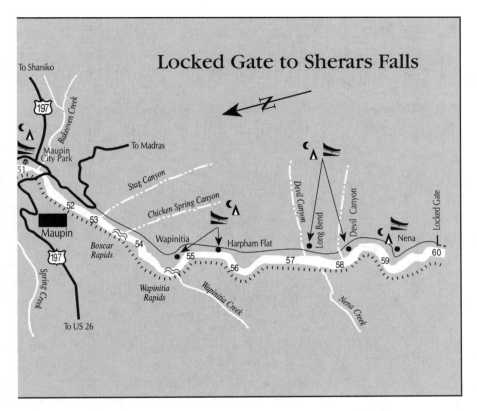

Locked Gate to Sherars Falls

sign for "Deschutes River Rec Area." Just past (0.3 mile) Maupin City Park, turn left onto the access road. This road is paved 7.7 miles to the Sherars Bridge junction (SR 216).

Getting Downriver from Sherars Bridge. For access below Sherars Bridge, take SR 216 (this is a right turn if you are travelling down from Maupin) and go east 0.5 mile from the junction with the access road from Maupin. Turn left onto the Deschutes River Access Road (there is a sign). This road continues another 16.8 miles to Macks Canyon.

It is possible to walk downstream for part or all of the 24 miles from Macks Canyon to the mouth of the river. If you are going to do this, park your car out of the way on the broad hairpin turn just as the road drops into the campground. The trail takes off through the sage brush at this point and soon merges with the old railroad grade. For the first four miles, the railroad ties were left in place, but the rails and trestles were removed. This means the old grade is difficult walking in places due to the ties, various rock slides that cover parts of the trail, and sage brush

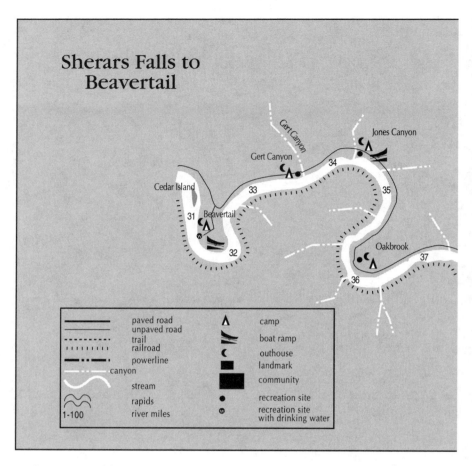

Sherars Falls to Beavertail

Jones Canyon

Gert Canyon

Gert Canyon

34

Cedar Island

33

35

31 Beavertail

32

Oakbrook

36

37

paved road		camp	
unpaved road		boat ramp	
trail		outhouse	
railroad		landmark	
powerline		community	
canyon			
stream		recreation site	
rapids		recreation site with drinking water	
1-100 river miles			

and occasional barbed wire fences that have grown in the middle of the grade. In addition, the lack of trestles means you have to climb down, then up, several steep gullies. Still, it is a nice walk high above the river. Here you can find solitude, admire fine views of the river, and contemplate things like, "My, my. Isn't this rock slide swell habitat for rattlesnakes!" After four miles, the road bed is clear and maintained all the way to the mouth of the river.

For reasons which should be clear by now, downstream bicycle access from Macks Canyon is not good. It is possible to ride/carry a bike through here. It is also possible to climb Mt. Everest, but that doesn't mean everyone could or should do it.

There are also some rough trails that meander next to the river downstream from Macks Canyon campground.

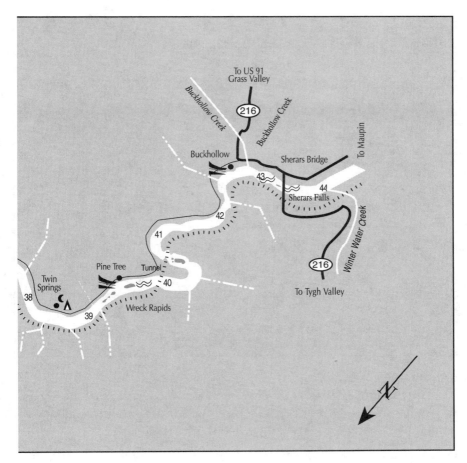

Camps and Recreation Sites—Maupin to Locked Gate

The camping and recreation sites in this section are on the access road leading south from Maupin; see above for directions. Campgrounds are similar to one another: most have a sign on the road announcing the name of the campground, all are on the river and offer some shady places, but none are developed like Trout Creek, Beavertail, etc., and none have water.

Camp in previously established campsites, and do not drive off the road or onto vegetation. Each campground has its own fee station. As stated in Chapter 2, a 1993 rule limits the size of groups in this area to 24 people or less.

These camps tend to be oriented to rafters and large groups, since many rafting parties begin their trip here. Most of the camps have places

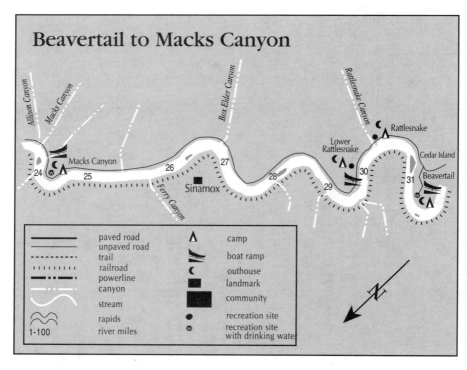

Beavertail to Macks Canyon

Legend:

paved road	
unpaved road	
trail	
railroad	
powerline	
canyon	
stream	
rapids	
1-100	river miles
Λ	camp
	boat ramp
☾	outhouse
■	landmark
▮	community
●	recreation site
Ⓦ	recreation site with drinking water

Map labels: Allison Canyon, Macks Canyon, Box Elder Canyon, Rattlesnake Canyon, Rattlesnake, Lower Rattlesnake, Cedar Island, Beavertail, Macks Canyon, Sinamox, Ferry Canyon, 24, 25, 26, 27, 28, 29, 30, 31

to assemble a raft and launch it.

The road mileages listed below are from the junction of the access road with US 197. Drift miles (DM) are measured from the boat launch near Warm Springs, and river miles (RM) from the mouth.

Locked Gate. 6.9 miles from US 197. DM 36.9/RM 60.0

There is no sign, but when you reach a locked gate on the road you are there. Park off the road for walk-in access above the Locked Gate. There are no camping or other facilities at this site.

Nena. 6.1 miles from US 197; sign on road. DM 37.7/RM 59.2.

This is the furthest upstream launch site before the Locked Gate. *Camping:* Some tent sites are in grassy areas near the river and shade trees. Some have tables. There are good RV sites at the north and south ends. Fee is $3.00 per night. *Facilities:* One outhouse; garbage cans; four tables; good gravel boat launch, although maneuvering room is tight if you have a trailer; trailer parking is poor. No water.

Devil's Canyon. 5.0 miles from US 197; sign on road. DM 38.7/RM 58.2.

Camping: This is a small campground, but there is space for a large group at the north end. There is little shade for campers, however. Some sites have tables. Fee is $3.00 per night. *Facilities:* One outhouse; garbage cans near outhouse; three tables. No water or boat launch.

Long Bend. 4.4 miles from US 197; sign on road. DM 39.8/RM 57.1.

This campground is scheduled to have major changes in 1993. What is described here is Long Bend before any changes took place. *Camping:* There are numerous places to camp in this long, strung-out campground. The north end has several sites near the river and shade trees. These are in a sandy area, so be careful not to get your car stuck. The south end, which is a rocky drive far from the outhouse, has a flat area that can accommodate a large group, however there is little shade. There is a rough boat launch at this end. Camping fee is $3.00 per night. *Facilities:* Outhouse across the road from the campground; garbage cans; three tables; rough boat launch at south end. No water.

Harpham Flat (also know as Dutchman Flat). 3.4 miles from US 197; sign on road. DM 41.4/RM 55.5.

This is a popular launching point for boats and rafts. It is also the primary take-out point for hard boats coming down the river from Warm

There are several locked gates along the Deschutes, but this is THE Locked Gate. It is 6.9 miles south of Maupin. Foot traffic only is permitted beyond the gate.

Harpham Flat on a busy weekend. (BLM photo)

Springs or Trout Creek. Near the ramp, there is a large parking area suitable for lots of trailers. *Camping:* A large, shadeless flat area at the north end has enough tent room for a medium-sized traveling circus. Large groups will be well accommodated here. No camping fee. *Facilities:* Four outhouses, two near the boat ramp and two near the camping area; garbage cans near boat ramp and also near camping; good gravel boat ramp. No water or tables.

Wapinitia. 2.9 miles from US 197; sign on road. DM 42.1/RM 54.8.

The bank is low here; the beach is shallow and rocky with quiet water; and the good whitewater starts just downstream. In addition, although this area is not as large as Harpham Flat, it offers more room for assembling rafts. For these reasons, Wapinitia has long been a favorite put-in for rafters. *Camping:* Several shady tent sites among the trees near the river. Some sites have a table. There is a dirt area across the road that can be used if the campground is full. In general, however, large groups should not camp at Wapinitia. Fee is $3.00 per night. *Facilities:* Two outhouses; garbage cans; two tables; two good raft launching areas, but not as good for hard boats. Trailer parking is poor. No water.

Camps and Recreation Sites—Maupin to Sherars Bridge

The campgrounds in this section are primitive (except for Maupin City Park) and similar to those above Maupin. Recreation sites and campgrounds in this area are used primarily as termination points for raft trips, and for steelhead and trout fishing. As stated earlier, a 1993 rule limits the size of groups in this segment to 24 people or less. There is a fee station at each campground.

Other than Maupin City Park, all road mileages given here are mea-

> *"Our goal is to maintain and improve the Deschutes as a resource for the present and future. Our challenge is to do this while balancing and respecting often conflicting uses, mixed land ownerships, and differing value systems."* Jim Hancock, district manager, Bureau of Land Management.

sured from the beginning of the Deschutes River Access Road at its junction with the Bakeoven Road. Drift miles (DM) are measured from the boat ramp at Warm Springs, and river miles (RM) from the mouth.

Maupin City Park. DM 45.4/RM 51.5.

This park has both picnic and camping facilities. The green lawns, large shade trees, and river access make it a pleasant place to stop or stay. *Camping:* You will find a large number of sites for either tents ($6.00 per day) or RVs ($12.00 per day for full hookup). *Facilities:* Water; toilets; garbage cans; tables; boat ramp.

Oasis. 0.9 mile from junction; sign on road. DM 46.4/RM 50.5.

This is a long campground, extending about a quarter mile north from the entry. Oasis is scheduled for major renovations in 1993. The description here is Oasis at the end of 1992. *Camping:* Several sites are in grassy areas, and some are near the river and have shade; $3.00 fee per night. *Facilities:* Two outhouses at north end; garbage cans; six tables. No water or boat launch.

Grey Eagle. 1.6 miles from junction; sign on road. DM 47.1/RM 49.8.

Grey Eagle will probably be converted to day-use only in 1993 or 1994. *Camping:* A few camping sites are here, but this is one of the smaller campgrounds. *Facilities:* Outhouse across the road; garbage cans; one table. No water or boat launch.

Blue Hole/Handicap Ramp. 3.1 miles from junction; sign on the road for "Blue Hole." DM 48.6/RM 48.3.

This unique facility has a parking lot suitable for wheelchair transport vehicles and a fishing ramp for handicapped anglers. Wheelchair access is good to the ramp, picnic area, and outhouse. Anyone may fish here, but handicapped anglers have priority, so even if you were there first, make adequate room if someone comes in a wheelchair. Handicapped anglers may reserve a campsite by calling 503-395-2270.

Camping: Overnight camping is not permitted in the picnic area south of the handicapped ramp. However, you may camp on the flat area just north of the ramp. Fee is $3.00 per night. *Facilities:* Handicap access for fishing; outhouse suitable for wheelchairs; garbage cans; eight tables. No water or boat launch.

Oak Springs. 3.5 miles from junction; sign on road. DM 49.0/RM 47.9.

The Oak Springs area is sometimes used as a raft termination point because the Oak Springs Rapids (Class IV) are avoided. There are unmarked places to camp on either side of this campground. The area to the north has two tables and is known as Surf City because the nearby standing waves are a popular place for kayakers to improve their skills. The unmarked area just south of here is the best place to pull-out a boat. *Camping:* There are several places for tents, but RVs may also find this a good place because it is flat and the road access is good. There is no shade. Fee is $3.00 per night. *Facilities:* Outhouse; garbage cans; three tables; waste water sump near garbage cans; take-out area for boats south of main camping area. No water.

White River. 4.8 miles from junction; no sign. DM 50.3/RM 46.6.

Owned and administered by the CTWS. *Camping:* Rather a barren, rocky, shadeless area for tent camping, although RVs may find it suitable. No camping fee. *Facilities:* Outhouse; garbage cans. No water, tables, or boat launch.

Sandy Beach. 6.0 miles from junction; no sign. DM 51.5/RM 45.4.

Owned and administered by the CTWS. This is the best place to pull out a raft or boat before Sherars Falls because it is a larger, less congested area than at Sherars (see below). There is a quiet beach near an island, and young children may find this a good place for wading and cooling off. However, keep cars, lawn chairs, beach blankets, and children out of the landing area. This has been a problem on some busy weekends. *Camping:* Overnight camping is not permitted here. *Facilities:* Two outhouses; garbage cans; broad sandy beach for landing boats and rafts. No water or tables.

Sandy Beach, where many white water adventures end.

Sherars Falls. 7.2 miles from junction.

This land is owned and administered by the CTWS. There is a raft pull-out 0.4 mile above Sherars Bridge on the west bank, but it can get crowded. Sandy Beach is a better place to pull-out. Also, the Sherars landing may be closed sometime soon, so forming a habit of taking out at Sandy Beach is a good idea. *Camping:* During the salmon season, many people park RVs in the area near the bridge. This area is extremely rocky and is unsuitable for tent camping. *Facilities:* Portable toilets; garbage cans. No water or tables.

Sherars Falls is at the cross road of Highway 216 and the river access roads, as well as the cross road of two cultures. (Photo courtesy ODFW)

Camps and Recreation Sites— Sherars Bridge to Macks Canyon

There are two developed campgrounds in this area: Beavertail and Macks Canyon. All other campgrounds are semi-developed and similar to those upstream. Each campground has its own fee station.

These campgrounds are primarily used by steelhead anglers, with some limited trout fishing activity. If you are looking for solitude and an alternative to the flesh pots of the Maupin area, come here any time other than the peak steelhead season (August and September).

All road mileages given here are measured from the beginning of this section of the Deschutes River Access Road, at its junction with SR 216. Drift miles (DM) are measured from the boat ramp at Warm Springs, and river miles (RM) from the mouth.

Buckhollow. 0.5 mile from junction; no sign. DM 54.2/RM 42.7.

This is the first launching point after Sherars Falls. A steep dirt road

Some boat launches, like this one at Buckhollow, are rough and require backing a trailer over bankside boulders.

leads to the water, and boats may be launched at the shallow beach. After launching, drive your rig back up to the main road and park it there, even if you expect a shuttle driver to pick it up later. There is simply not enough room to leave rigs at the launch area. There are no campsites here, camping is not permitted, and there are no facilities except the launch.

Pine Tree. 2.9 miles from junction; sign on road. DM 57.4/RM39.5.

This boat launching site is popular because it is below Wreck Rapids (Class III). The boat ramp is gravel, but the road leading to it is rough. Parking is limited. *Camping:* Camping is not permitted here. *Facilities:* garbage cans; one table; boat launch. No water or outhouse.

Twin Springs. 4.0 miles from junction; sign on road. DM 58.5/RM 38.4.

Camping: There is a large flat area suitable for tents, but little shade; $3.00 fee per night. *Facilities:* Two outhouses; garbage cans; one table; waste water sump near outhouse. No water or boat launch.

Oak Brook. 6.3 miles from junction; sign on road. DM 61.1/RM 35.8.

Camping: This is a small, barren campground, although there is one shady campsite straight down the road from the entrance; $3.00 fee per night. *Facilities:* Two outhouses in the junipers at the north end; garbage cans on road; one table under a pathetic dead juniper. No water or boat launch.

Jones Canyon. 7.8 miles from junction; sign on road. DM 62.6/RM 34.3.

The rough boat launch that was here in the past is scheduled for removal in 1993. *Camping:* A few tent sites near the river have shade trees. Other sites are tucked away in the grass and sage brush. Fee is $3.00 per night. *Facilities:* Two outhouses; garbage cans; two tables. No water or boat launch.

Gert Canyon. 8.5 miles from junction; sign on road. DM 63.3/RM 33.6.

Camping: Several shady camping sites with tables; $3.00 fee per night. *Facilities:* Two outhouses; garbage cans; three tables; waste water sump near outhouses. No water or boat launch.

Beavertail. 9.6 miles from junction to turn-off. DM 65.4/RM 31.5.

There is a sign on the road for the turn-off; the campground is one mile down this road. *Camping:* This is a large, developed campground with extensive facilities and about 20 designated campsites, most of which have a table. There is a pay station as you enter the campground; $3.00 fee per night. *Facilities:* Water at three hand pump stations: one near the entrance, another at the north end of the campground, and one toward the south end. Six outhouses; garbage cans; tables at most designated campsites; waste water sumps near sites 4 and 9, and near the south outhouse. Good gravel boat launch with parking area above it; this is near the north-most outhouse. There is a sandy launch area near the entrance, but it is a good place to get stuck and is not recommended for trailers.

Upper Rattlesnake. 10.3 miles from junction; sign on road. DM 66.5/RM 30.4

Camping: Several shady sites with tables are near the river; $3.00 fee per night. *Facilities:* Two outhouses; garbage cans; four tables; waste water sump between outhouses and garbage cans. No water or boat launch.

Lower Rattlesnake. 10.6 miles from junction; no sign. DM 66.8/RM 30.1.

Camping: A few sites are near the river and have a little shade; $3.00 fee per night. *Facilities:* One outhouse; garbage cans; two tables. No water or boat launch.

Macks Canyon. 16.8 miles from junction; sign as you enter. DM 72.7/RM 24.2.

The road ends at Macks Canyon. From this point downstream, the only access is by boat or by foot on the old railroad bed; see the section above on access downriver from Maupin. *Camping:* Like Beavertail, this is a large, developed campground with extensive facilities and about 19 designated campsites with tables. The pay station is between campsites 4B and 5; $3.00 fee per night. *Facilities:* Water faucets scattered throughout the campground ; four outhouses; garbage cans; tables at designated campsites, plus a few for day use; two waste water sumps; good gravel boat launch; parking for trailers is above the launch area.

6

Macks Canyon
to the Columbia River

The part of the river between Macks Canyon and the Columbia River can be quite crowded. It can also be deserted. During the steelhead season (Mid-July to October) it gets the heaviest fishing pressure of anywhere on the Deschutes. The lowest ten miles can be especially busy at this time, but throughout the rest of the year this can be a place of solitude. Trout fishing in this area is poor, relative to the fishing on the upper half of the river, but a few sizeable fish can still be found, and the fishing pressure is lower.

While the last few miles of the river offer some good rapids, including the Class IV Rattlesnake, and Class III Colorado, most boaters don't come down here for whitewater thrills. The low gradient during much of the drift makes for dull boating and a lot of rowing. On the other hand, it makes for good steelhead holding water. Because there are some tricky rapids at the end of the ride, anglers who drift this part of the river need to be skilled boat handlers.

This segment of the river is very popular with jet boaters. Since most jet boats put in at Heritage Landing, they have to negotiate several tough rapids and riffles before getting to the prime steelhead water. Therefore, they need to be skilled operators of their craft and knowledgeable of the rapids.

Other than Macks Canyon, which is covered in the preceding chapter, there are two drive-in access points in this area: Kloan and the mouth of the river. These are described below. Following that section is a description of the boat-in campsites between Macks Canyon and the mouth.

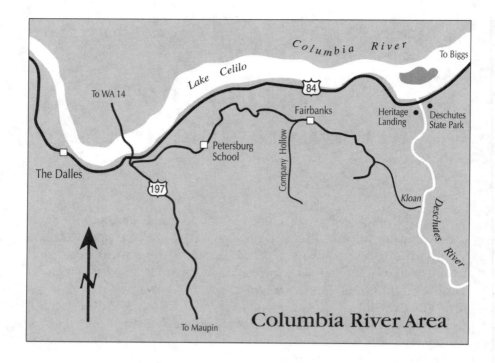

Columbia River Area

Kloan

If your vehicle does not have good road clearance and a four-wheel drive "low" setting, *don't go to Kloan*.

Getting There. The most straight forward route to Kloan begins just outside The Dalles, near where US 197 intersects I-84. *From I-84:* Take exit 87 to the south and follow the directions for getting to Kloan from US 197 south-bound. *From US 197 Southbound:* Cross the bridge over the railroad tracks, and turn right where there is a sign for The Dalles; turn right again at the stop sign. *From US 197 Northbound:* Look for a large sign pointing right for Yakima, and left for The Dalles; bear left and turn right at the stop sign.

You should now be on a road that heads east and parallels I-84. There is a sign for "Petersburg School." If you are on the correct road, you will soon pass a large motel, The Inn at The Dalles. This road turns right and is known as Fifteenmile Road.

After 3.0 miles from the US 197 intersection there is a fork; bear left. After 3.6 miles you pass through the tiny community of Petersburg School. After 8.7 miles you pass through the even smaller community of

Fairbanks. At 12.5 miles, turn left onto Fulton Road, which is gravel. Up to this point there has been only one road sign for Kloan. Maybe they don't want you to get there.

Fulton Road forks in 1.6 miles. Take the right fork, which is a broad, well-graded dirt road. You should see an ominous sign stating, "Not Maintained for Winter Travel/Use At Own Risk." The sign means that after a heavy rain the road surface has as much traction as marbles dipped in hot grease.

The road is broad and flat for the next 2.2 miles to the canyon rim. When you reach the canyon rim, stop and pick up a large rock. Roll it down the sheer precipice of the canyon. Watch it gather speed and carom off other rocks, eventually shattering into smithereens so nothing remains but a fading echo in the remote and lonely canyon. Think to yourself: "That could be my car. I could be in it." Maybe you should walk.

For the next 1.2 miles the road drops about 1000 vertical feet to the river. Shift into four-wheel low to save your brakes. There is a gate on the road. If it was closed when you reached it, be sure to close it behind you. You may also need to get out and move large rocks that have rolled onto the road.

At the bottom there is a fork in the road. Take either fork, and park somewhere near the railroad tracks. From here, it is a short walk down the bank to the river.

River access is similar to that from Heritage Landing (see below). You may camp at Kloan, but there are no facilities—probably because they didn't expect anyone to make it down the road alive.

Deschutes River State Park/Heritage Landing

These twin facilities are managed by the Oregon State Parks and Recreation Department. They are across the river from each other, just up from the confluence with the Columbia River.

Getting There. Eastbound on I-84, take exit 97 (Celilo/Deschutes State Park). After 2.7 miles, you will reach the river. *Westbound on I-84,* take exit 105 (Biggs), and follow the signs for the park. It is 4.3 miles down the frontage road. *From US 97,* either north-bound or south-bound, follow the signs from Biggs, as above.

The State Park is on the east bank, and Heritage Landing is on the west bank.

Camping and Facilities at the State Park. The park is nicely maintained, with many shade trees and a large grassy area. It is a pleasant oasis on hot summer days. There are places to picnic here, as well as places to camp.

By State Park standards, this is rated as a "primitive" campground, although by Deschutes River standards it's like staying at The Ritz. RVs up to 30 feet can be accommodated, but there are no hookups. All camping is in 34 designated sites, plus 24 overflow sites. There are no reservations, and at the height of the steelhead season (August through mid-September) it can be difficult to get a site. There is a $9.00 fee per night. The State Park is open for camping from mid-March to early November; the rest of the year it is open for day use only.

Facilities include drinking water, toilets, and garbage cans. *Do not* take out rafts or boats at the park; go across the river to Heritage Landing.

River Access from the State Park. Just outside the park entrance, there is a trail suitable for hiking or mountain biking. An experiment with low-impact, early season horse access will be started in 1993. No other forms of travel are permitted. You may walk or bike all the way to Macks Canyon on this trail, although 20 miles upstream it becomes all but impassable for a mountain bike (see the comments in Chapter 5).

Facilities at Heritage Landing. Heritage Landing is the launch site for power boats, as well as the landing site for drift craft. The concrete ramp is only for those with trailers. It can get quite busy at the height of the season, so be prepared to load/unload very quickly. Rafts should land on the sandy beach adjacent to the concrete ramp. There is a hose between the two landing areas; you may use it to clean up your raft or boat. Because it gets so busy here, there is a 15 minute maximum for loading and unloading.

With its broad green lawns and large shade trees, the Deschutes River State Park is a pleasant oasis on a hot day.

Heritage Landing has a trash dumpster behind a wooden screen next to the ramp. There are also rest rooms here (with toilets that flush!). Parking for those with boat trailers is in a gravel lot across the road. A parking area for day-users is just up the road from the boat landing.

The Deschutes River State Park is at the mouth of the river. RVs and trailers are accommodated here, but there are no hookups.

You may not camp at Heritage Landing.

River Access from Heritage Landing. About 200 yards from the day use parking area (see above) you will see the trail that goes up the river. You can travel this trail for a long way, however you will begin encountering barbed wire fences after the first couple of miles. Also, the trail is tough to walk in areas where the bank is steep. For these reasons, many anglers walk along the railroad tracks until they reach their favorite water. See Chapter 2 for a discussion of private property issues regarding the railroad tracks.

Boat-in Campsites

River miles (RM) are measured from the confluence with the Columbia. Drift miles (DM) are measured from the boat ramp at Warm Springs. By convention, "West" refers to the left bank when facing downstream; "East" refers to the right bank when facing downstream. See Chapter 2 for further discussion of boat-in camping.

DM 74.3/RM 22.6 (East) After leaving Macks Canyon campground, the river makes a long left turn, and you come to a group of islands. The standard passage is to the right of the first one, and to the left of the second. About 200 feet below these islands a flat appears on the right bank.

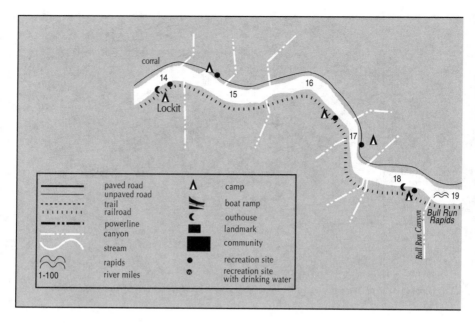

Campsites can be found for the next few hundred yards downstream, although it is hard to find ones that are both shady and rock-free. There is no outhouse here.

DM 74.8/RM 22.1 (West) Along the railroad tracks on the left side of the river, you see a white sign with "Dike" on it. About 150 yards downstream from this sign there is a grassy flat with an outhouse. There is no shade here, but a fine steelhead run glides past the camp.

DM 75.5/RM 21.4 (East) After drifting through a small rapids, you enter a straight stretch of flat water, ending in a sharp left turn that can be seen ahead. About half way between the small rapids and this turn, there is an open grassy area on a gentle hill on the right side. Good flat tent sites can be found near the river, but not much shade. An outhouse is located up the hill.

DM 76.2/ RM 20.7 (East) There is a flat on the right bank as the river makes a 180-degree right turn. Beginning at the mid-point of this turn, there are numerous tent sites shaded by alders. An outhouse is located part way up the hill.

DM 76.7/RM 20.2 (East) A face of columnar basalt rises out of the river on the right. Although the paint has faded, you can still make out the

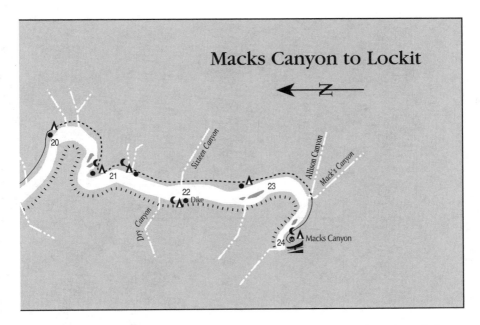

Macks Canyon to Lockit

two foot high inscription "Nookie Rock" near the base of this basalt face. The reasons for this notation are left to the imagination of the reader.

Below Nookie Rock, a large gravel bar forms in mid-river. About a quarter mile past this, a flat opens on the left. Opposite this flat on the right you can find space for a few tents in the trees. There is no outhouse.

DM 78.8/ RM 18.1 (West) About a quarter mile below Bull Run Rapids, a broad grassy flat develops on the left. There is plenty of camping here, and an outhouse, but shade is scarce. Both sides of the river have excellent fishing.

DM 79.8/RM 17.1 (East) The river begins a long straight stretch. The flat on the right offers a few tent sites, but no outhouse.

DM 80.1/RM 16.8 (West) There is a flat behind bankside alders. A few tent sites can be found. There is no outhouse.

DM 82.2/RM 14.7 (East) After passing through a Class II rapids, you come to a long straight stretch before Lockit. During the steelhead season, there are several elaborate campsites on the left bank beginning at RM 15.5. These are on private property. Although camping is not permitted here, it is OK to fish. On the right bank, at around RM 14.7, there

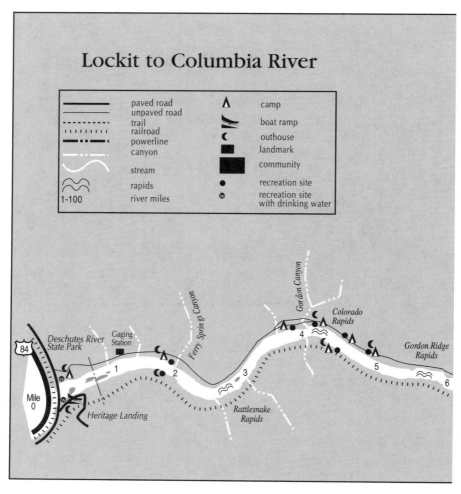

Lockit to Columbia River

———————	paved road	ʌ	camp
	unpaved road		boat ramp
- - - - - - - -	trail		
ı ı ı ı ı ı ı ı ı	railroad	C	outhouse
—·—·—·—	powerline	■	landmark
	canyon		community
	stream	•	recreation site
1-100	rapids	ⓦ	recreation site with drinking water
	river miles		

are a few sites in the alders, but no outhouse.

DM 82.7/RM 14.2 (West) As you drift though a small rapids, a flat appears on the left as the river makes a long left sweep. At the end of the rapids, some tent sites can be seen in the trees at the beginning of the flat, however there are better sites about 300 yards downstream. Some of these are in the trees, some on the grassy flat above them. There is an outhouse in the middle of the flat. This area is called "Lockit."

DM 84.7/RM 12.2 (West) As the river approaches Harris Canyon, it makes a near 180-degree left turn. In the middle of this turn, just past a riffle, you can see some campsites on the left bank flat. If you keep

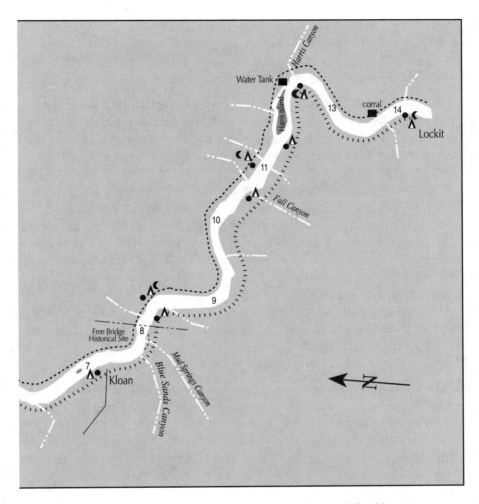

going around the bend another quarter mile, you will find better camp-sites and boat landings. The outhouse is at this north end, almost oppo-site Harris Canyon.

DM 85.6/RM 11.3 (West) Following Harris Canyon, you pass through two rapids. The second rapids marks the northern end of Harris Island (barely discernible as an island). Following this rapids, a large flat de-velops on the right, and a smaller one on the left. There are a few camp-sites on the left flat, but no outhouse. At this point the right flat is too rocky for good camping, but things improve downstream a bit (see below).

DM 85.9/RM 11.0 (East) As you proceed down the flat described above, a long row of alders ends with three very large trees—about twice as tall as the others. There is a good campsite here with an outhouse. More shade trees have been planted and are well established.

DM 86.2/RM 10.7 (West) The flat water ends, and the river turns right and forms a small riffle. A long (over a mile) flat opens on the left. You may camp on this flat, or anywhere for the next three miles, as long as cattle are not present. Fires are not allowed at any time of year. There is no outhouse.

This flat, and the flats below it—about three miles of river bank—have no riparian zone whatsoever, and you may wonder if this land was used for testing nuclear weapons or storing toxic waste. No. Cows did this. This land, known as Kortge Flat, is now owned by the State of Oregon. However, a previous owner retains historical grazing rights and continues to put cattle on the land. The State does not presently have authority to prevent this.

It is abusive grazing practice like this that gives even responsible ranchers—and there are many—a bad name, and increases the public pressure to enact tough grazing laws on private land. Citizens of Oregon, take a good look at this cow-blasted landscape. You own it.

DM 88.3/RM 8.6 (East) As the river sweeps right, a flat opens up on the right. Keep going to the downstream end of this flat. An old railroad car cabin sits up the hill. The campsites are a few hundred feet upstream from the old cabin. An outhouse is located about 200 feet from the river. Numerous tent sites can be found in the grassy area, but there is not much shade. Shade trees have been planted, offering hope for the future.

> *"Many citizens over the years have unselfishly donated their time and money so that you, too, can enjoy this wonderful river. The Oregon State Parks and Recreation Department asks all persons to leave in passing no mark upon the land that might diminish its value for another, for the unspoiled beauty of these waterways—of value to the human spirit—is the common heritage of all."* Oregon State Parks and Recreation Department.

DM 88.7/RM 8.2 (West)
You can see power lines crossing the river ahead. About 300 yards upstream from the power lines there is a small camping area without an outhouse.

On this part of the river, jet boats are a common sight.

DM 89.9/RM 7.0 (West)
About a quarter mile after Freebridge, an island can be seen on the right. On the left, opposite this island, is the beginning of the area called "Kloan." There are several good tent sites scattered along the left bank for several hundred yards. There is no outhouse at Kloan.

DM 92.2/RM 4.7 (East) After Gordon Ridge Rapids, but about three-quarters of a mile above Colorado Rapids, a flat develops on the right. Look downstream to see lava cliffs looming above the road bed. You might also spot a road that cuts down to the river from the main road above. Almost to the start of the cliffs, and about one-fourth mile downstream from where the road cuts down, there is an outhouse. There is good camping here amid tall grass and short trees.

DM 92.4/RM 4.5 (West) About one-quarter mile below the spot described above, on the left side, there is good camping. The outhouse is up the bank in the middle of the camping area. Look on the right bank for a culvert that comes out from under the access road; the outhouse is opposite this culvert. Some sites here have shade.

DM 92.4/RM 4.5 (East) Opposite the site described above and about 200 yards downstream from the culvert, there is a nice tent site in the trees. There is no outhouse, but it is a short walk upstream to reach one (see description at RM 4.7).

DM 92.9/RM 4.0 (East) About 200 yards below Colorado Rapids, on the right side, you can see an outhouse about 100 feet up the hill from the river. There is a flat near the outhouse that offers good camping in the grass. Shade trees have been planted here, but most have died.

Heritage Landing has separate areas for boats and rafts. There is a trash dumpster behind this sign.

DM 93.1/RM 3.8 (East) As you approach the boulder strewn area known as Madden Riffle, there is a flat on the right with numerous tent sites. There is no shade or outhouse here.

DM 95.2/RM 1.9 (East) Flats open on both sides of the river about 200 yards below the rapids at Ferry Springs Canyon. There is an outhouse and a nice tent site in the trees.

DM 95.1/RM 1.8 (West) Opposite the site described above there is an outhouse. This is primarily a pit stop and not a campsite.

DM 96.6/RM 0.3 (East) The Deschutes River State Park appears on the right. Do not take out boats and rafts at the park. Instead, use Heritage Landing on the west side. In this area, there is a 5 mph speed limit for all water craft. While this poses little problem for rafts and drift boats, power boats should observe the speed limit.

DM 96.7/RM 0.2 (West) Heritage Landing appears on the left. The ramp is for trailers, while rafts should use the sandy beach adjacent to the ramp. See above for a description of Heritage Landing and its facilities.

7

Fishing the Deschutes

The Deschutes River is unique among North American fisheries because it offers world-class fishing for both rainbow trout and steelhead. If this were not enough, there is a strong run of spring chinook salmon. The river's rich and diverse ecology makes outstanding trout and steelhead fishing possible, but it could not continue without catch-and-release regulations and wild fish management.

This chapter covers subjects of interest to all Deschutes anglers, regardless of which species of fish they pursue. These subjects include fishing regulations, wading, and releasing fish. Chapter 8 covers how to fish for Deschutes rainbow trout, while Chapter 9 discusses steelhead and salmon fishing on the river.

Fishing Regulations (1993)

The fishing regulations listed here are current in 1993. They are offered as a guideline, but anglers should always refer to the official regulations for the "gospel." Also, regulations can change during the year. For example, the fall salmon season has been closed the last few years.

Terminal tackle. Barbless flies and lures only except bait may be used with barbless hooks from Sherars Falls downstream to the upper trestle (about three miles). In this area, commercially canned fish may be used for bait.

Seasons
Opening Day is the fourth Saturday in April.
Steelhead: April 1 to December 31 from the mouth to Sherars Falls; Opening Day to December 31 above Sherars Falls.
Salmon: April 1 to October 31 below Sherars Falls. Opening Day to October 31 above Sherars Falls. No salmon may be taken when fishing the six mile stretch of special permit water on the Warm Springs Reservation.

Trout: all year, except where noted below.

Whitefish, other species: all year, except where noted below.

Special seasonal restriction: from the northern boundary of the Warm Springs Reservation (near river mile 69) to Pelton Dam, the following restrictions apply: No angling of any kind from November 1 to Opening Day, except steelhead may be taken from November 1 to December 31.

Catch limits

Trout: 2 per day, 10 inch minimum and 13 inch maximum length.

Steelhead and salmon: 2 per day in any combination; 6 per 7 consecutive days. Only adipose-clipped steelhead may be taken. All others must be released unharmed.

Rainbow trout over 20 inches in length are considered steelhead.

No angling from a floating device (boat, raft, float tube, etc.). The angler must be grounded.

No angling from Pelton Regulating Dam downstream about 600 feet to ODFW markers.

Warm Springs Permits. The lower Deschutes River borders the Warm Springs Reservation from Pelton Dam to about river mile 69 (between Dixon and Hardy). This is a distance of nearly 31 miles, and it is completely off-limits to anyone who is not a member of the Confederated Tribes of the Warm Springs Reservation. You may not land a boat, walk, camp, or fish here. This includes all islands west of mid-river (these are posted by the CTWS). The only exception is a six-mile stretch from the locked gate at Dry Creek campground to the Wasco/Jefferson county line, a point opposite the Trout Creek campground. A special permit is required to fish for trout or steelhead in this section, and to camp at Dry Creek. Salmon fishing is not permitted. Other special regulations are detailed on the Warm Springs permit.

Warm Springs permits may be purchased for the season or on a daily basis. All persons, regardless of age, must have a permit to fish or otherwise access this area. To be valid, the permit must be kept on your person, and you must also have a current Oregon Angling License, even if you are not an Oregon resident.

Kinds of fish

There are many species of fish in the Deschutes, but there are eight that an angler might catch: rainbow trout, summer steelhead, chinook salmon (spring and fall runs), mountain whitefish, bull trout, northern squawfish, suckers, and chiselmouth. Each of these species is described briefly below. Chapters 8 and 9 discuss trout, steelhead, and salmon in more detail.

All eight species are native to the Deschutes, and evolved together. Each species fills an ecological niche, and none of them should be wasted or treated disdainfully. Only two species—spring chinook salmon and steelhead—are supplemented with stocking from hatcheries, and even these species have sizable populations of wild fish.

Wild Fish. Wild fish are native to the river and naturally reproduce here. Wild fish compared to hatchery fish are what real life is compared to TV sitcoms. Wild fish are hardier, healthier, and stronger (and offer more sport). The wild trout, steelhead, salmon, and other fish of the Deschutes are a precious resource for the present, a unique heritage of the past, and an essential part of the future. Every angler who cherishes this river needs to be aware of the issues surrounding wild fish, and work for their preservation and enhancement.

Rainbow Trout. The rainbow trout of the Deschutes River are known as "redsides" because of their distinctive coloration. The typical redside that anglers catch is between 10 and 15 inches long and fights like a tiger. There are larger trout in the river, as well. Chapter 8 discusses these fish in more detail.

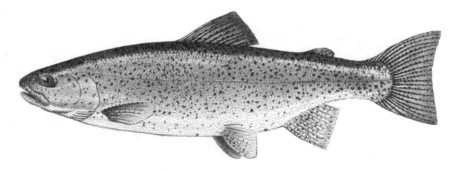

Deschutes River Rainbow Trout. (Courtesy ODFW)

Steelhead. Steelhead are migratory fish that are genetically identical to rainbow trout. Steelhead migrate to the ocean at an early age, feed and grow large there, and return to the river to spawn one or two years after they leave. Deschutes steelhead are generally five to eight pounds in weight. A number of steelhead bound for other rivers make a short visit into the Deschutes because of its cooler water. Most of these fish stay in the lower part of the river, and some of them are 15 to 20 pounds, or even more.

There is a sizable population of wild steelhead in the Deschutes, despite hatchery stocking. Chapter 9 has more information on steelhead.

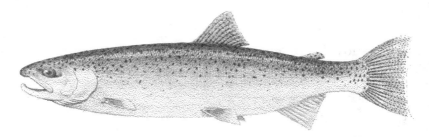

Deschutes River Steelhead. (Courtesy ODFW)

Chinook Salmon. There are two types of Deschutes River chinook salmon: spring chinook that enter the river beginning in April, and fall chinook that enter somewhat later. The salmon are typically 12-15 pounds, although 25-30 pound fish are not uncommon. Salmon are discussed further in Chapter 9.

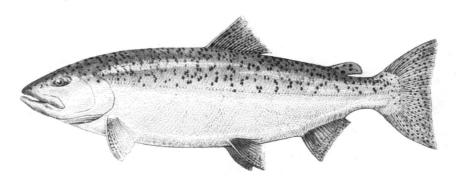

Chinook Salmon. (Courtesy ODFW)

Whitefish. Whitefish are the Rodney "don't get no respect" Dangerfield fish of the Deschutes. Compared to their trout cousins they are weak and ugly, and many believe them to be the consolation prize for not catching a trout.

Actually, properly prepared whitefish are good eating. They are excellent smoked. And catching whitefish is better than catching no fish. In cold water, whitefish are more active than trout, and during the winter months of December through February they can provide excellent sport on small nymphs. This can be a good time of year to hone your nymph fishing skills.

As you might expect from the shape of their small mouth, whitefish feed primarily on the bottom. They readily take nymphs fished deep, but rarely take a dry fly in the Deschutes. They are receptive to midge pupae fished just sub-surface in quiet water. If you are getting a lot of hits to your stonefly nymph, but few hookups, you may be in whitefish water. They can't always get your big stiff nymph imitation into their little mouth, but that doesn't stop them from trying.

Whitefish and trout evolved together, and while whitefish outnumber trout in the Deschutes by 3:1 or even 7:1, they do not compete directly. Being weaker swimmers than trout, they reside in slower water. Whitefish are not tolerant of polluted water, and a healthy whitefish population is an indication of good water quality.

Mountain Whitefish. (Courtesy ODFW)

Bull trout. Bull trout, formerly called Dolly Varden, are sometimes hooked in the upper part of the river. These fish can grow to five pounds or more. Many anglers have trouble distinguishing a bull trout from a brown trout, and sometimes you hear reports of "brown trout" in the lower Deschutes. Usually these turn out to be bull trout, but an occasional brown trout may "leak" down from Lake Simtustus. Bull trout populations are in jeopardy in Oregon, so release any you catch.

Bull Trout. (Courtesy ODFW)

Suckers. Suckers often live in fast water, where their trapezoidal shape helps hold them in one spot. Suckers outnumber trout by as much as 5:1 in the Deschutes, and anglers fishing deep nymphs sometimes snag one. A big sucker snagged in the dorsal fin in fast water can make you think you hooked the mother of all steelhead. Suckers feed mostly on plant material, but they will take stonefly nymphs, especially in winter. I once fair-hooked three suckers in one day in January. This was a new career high (or low).

Sucker. (Courtesy ODFW)

Northern Squawfish. Squawfish tend to be more populous in the lower river where the water is warmer. They have been known to take dry flies. The state of Oregon has a bounty program for Columbia River squawfish because they feed on juvenile salmon and steelhead in the slow-water pools behind the dams. In the Deschutes, however, squaw-fish are not a problem because the river is free-flowing below Pelton Dam. There is no need to try to rid the Deschutes of squawfish.

Squawfish. (Courtesy ODFW)

Chiselmouth. Chiselmouth look like a cross between a sucker and a squawfish. Sometimes when fishing for salmon, your bait can drift into a backeddy and be picked up by a chiselmouth.

Releasing fish

There are many reasons for releasing fish, even when not required by law. Before killing a fish, ask yourself: do I really need to eat this guy? wouldn't it be great if someone else could enjoy catching this fish, too? is my ego so fragile that I have to take this fish home as proof that I'm smarter than a pea-brained salmonid? Fresh fish can be a delicacy to eat, but there is usually more pleasure in catching them.

Here are some guidelines for releasing fish with minimum harm.

Use barbless hooks. It's the law on the Deschutes, and you'll hook (and land) more fish.

Use hooks smaller than size 2 on spoons and spinners. You will occa-sionally pick up trout with this gear, and large hooks will damage or kill them.

Don't play fish too long, especially during, just before, or just after the spring spawning season for trout and steelhead.

Use gear appropriate to the size of the fish. Rods that are too light, or leaders that are too thin, make you play fish to exhaustion. If you are fly fishing for trout, this means at least a 5 weight rod, and a tippet three pounds or heavier.

Wet your hands before handling fish.

If the water is warm (mid-July through mid-September) avoid touching the fish at all, in or out of the water. Leave it in the water and remove the hook with forceps or needle-nosed pliers. In warm water, bacteria and fungus grow quickly. Handling fish—with wet or dry hands, with or without cotton gloves—removes some of the slime coating that protects fish from bacteria and fungus. This is a much bigger problem in warm water than in cold.

The above advice about handling fish in warm water is especially important in the lower river. Here the water is warmer, and your most likely catch is a wild steelhead. Play it quickly and not to exhaustion, handle the fish as little as possible, and release it carefully after making sure it is well revived.

Back the hook out carefully with your fingers or forceps.

Don't squeeze the fish.

Don't hold it by the mouth.

Don't put your fingers in its gills.

Don't bang it on the rocks or pull it up on dry gravel.

If the fish is hooked any deeper than the lips, cut your leader, or if you are using hardware, cut the hook off the lure. Do this immediately; don't fiddle with it. The hook will soon work itself out without harm to the fish.

Don't get the fish all tangled up in your net. Better yet, don't use a net at all.

It is best to leave the fish in the water. If you need to take it out for a photo, keep it out of water for as little time as possible. Recent studies indicate that released fish are three times more likely to survive if they are left in the water than if they are taken out for even one minute.

If you need to hold the fish, as for a photo, grasp it in front of the tail with one hand, and support the head with the other. Your grip

Holding a fish prior to release.

will be more sure if you have a cotton glove on the grasping hand, or use a handkerchief. However, note the above warnings about handling fish in warm water.

Never drop a fish into fast water. If they start to tumble in the current, they may never regain their equilibrium, and will suffocate.

To revive a tired fish, grasp it in front of the tail, as described above, and keep it upright with its nose into the current (fish can't breathe unless water enters through their mouth). Some gentle current is helpful to get oxygen to the fish. If the water is fast, hold the fish downstream from your leg so your leg will break the current. Don't let go the first time the fish tries to escape, but wait for the second time. Make sure the gills are working before you let it go.

Use your leg to break the current when reviving a fish in swift water.

Wading

You can see them out there in midriver. Rising trout. BIG rising trout. They're beyond your casting range, but if you wade through that quiet water, then over those slippery rocks, then step gingerly through that fast riffle... How do you do all this without going for an unplanned swim? Or worse?

Proper gear for wading the Deschutes. A few simple tools and equipment can make your wading safer and more comfortable.

Hip boots tempt you into water that is too deep. They fill easily with water and are hard to get off in an emergency. Either use chest waders, or wade "wet" in a pair of quick-drying pants.

Anytime you wade, use waders or boots with felt soles. The rocks are slippery all year long. Many people even use boots with "corkers," little spikes that help grip the rocks.

Wear a belt around the outside of your waders so they will not fill as fast if you fall in. Even neoprene waders will fill, given enough time.

Use a wading staff—an old ski pole, a sturdy rake handle, or one made especially for wading. You are less likely to fall in, and even if you don't sink, falling in scares the fish. Don't clank the staff along the bottom—fish hear it. A rubber crutch tip can make your staff quieter.

Long underwear is more comfortable than jeans under waders. Polypropylene and similar synthetics are good because they are warm, form-fitting, and wick away perspiration.

Wading Wet. What could be simpler than wading wet? Just put on a pair of shorts and old sneakers and walk into the water, right? As proof that even the simplest of subjects can be made complicated, here are some points about wet wading in the Deschutes.

You risk a serious chilling, or even hypothermia, from cold water except in the height of summer. When you get chilled you might have trouble making your leg muscles work right, and this puts you at risk for a dunking. Also, wet wading may be uncomfortable in the cool of the evenings and mornings, even in summer.

Some parts of the river abound in poison ivy. If you wear shorts, be very careful around the banks of these areas.

Wear polypropylene or similar synthetic briefs. If you wear cotton briefs and get them wet, they can cause uncomfortable (and embarrassing) itch.

Wear shoes or boots that protect your ankles. The Deschutes is full of large, sharp boulders, and river sandals or low cut sneakers offer little protection for your ankles.

Consider wearing synthetic pants (available at many white water supply shops). These dry quickly and offer better protection from poison ivy and rocks. Complete the outfit with synthetic briefs or a swim suit underneath, and regular wading boots and polypropylene socks.

Wading Technique. The Deschutes is a good river to wade, but you should take a few precautions, described below.

Water is always deeper than you think. There are often deep pockets on the downstream side of boulders.

When wading through weed beds, you never know how deep the water is, but it is always deeper than you think.

Rocks are always more slippery than you think.

Quiet water on the Deschutes usually means the bottom will be soft silt, probably with weeds growing in it. The water looks less than two feet deep, but one step and you can find yourself up to your knees in mud, your waist in weeds, and your neck in water. Is any rising fish worth being stuck in the mud with water lapping at your chin?

The Deschutes is often quite deep right up to the bank. Look carefully before you get in, and make sure you know how deep it is. I have watched people take one step off the bank and leave nothing above the surface but a floating hat.

Before moving a foot, make sure the other foot is securely placed. Keep your feet close to the bottom to avoid stumbling on rocks or stepping in holes. Take small, slow steps, and feel ahead with your feet.

Move slowly and quietly so as not to disturb the fish. Try not to crunch rocks as you move; fish can hear you coming.

Keep yourself sideways to the current; you are more stable.

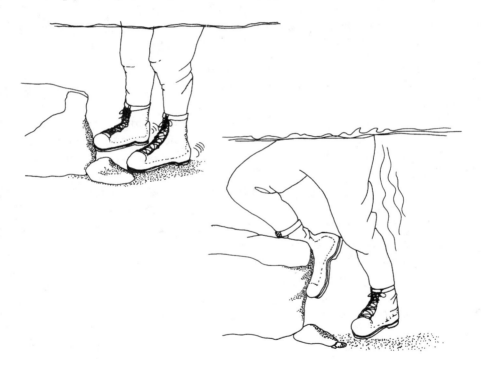

Left—Small steps close to bottom let you keep your balance and feel for rocks and holes. Right—Large, high steps set you up to stumble.

Don't cross your feet; this is an unstable position.

Be especially careful turning around. The most unstable position is when your back is to the flow; a heavy current surge could buckle your knees and set you adrift.

Climbing in or out of the water from a log can be dangerous because logs are often slippery and unstable. Look for something solid instead.

It's always easier to move downstream in fast water than upstream. When wading downstream think, "Can I get back upstream again?"

Look carefully when you wade. There might be a fish in your path. If you flush one out, don't worry about it. Come back later and fish that spot. He'll probably be back.

Walking backwards while wading is a really bad idea.

Sometimes you can steady yourself by hanging on to the overhanging branches of alders or other vegetation. But make sure that what you use for support is green and alive. If you use a dead branch for support—even one that is thick—it will likely break off in your hand.

Don't wade through spawning beds during April to July. Spawning beds are areas of fine gravel, usually less than one inch in diameter.

If you fall in and are carried downstream. The first rule is: *don't panic.* If your waders fill, they will make it hard to move your legs. But they will not "pull you under." Some other helpful tips.

If you fall into cold water, wrap your arms around your face and close your mouth tight. There is a reaction to cold water that tends to make a person gasp involuntarily, and that's not good when your mouth is under water.

Face downstream, on your back with your knees pulled up. Use your feet to cushion against rocks, and your arms to maneuver.

Don't let yourself be swept onto the upstream side of a large rock or log—you could be pinned to it by the current.

Don't stick a foot between two rocks where it might get wedged.

Grab an overhanging branch, if possible, and swing yourself up towards shore.

When in calmer water, swim for shore.

8

Fishing for Trout

On a sunny July afternoon the Deschutes River is saturated with light except near the bank, where the sunlight is filtered by outreaching alder branches. In these green-shadowed margins the river slides by neither fast nor slow, and its surface seems smooth and unbroken. The alders are alive with small, light brown caddisflies. They crawl on the underside of the leaves, sometimes make short flights in the open air, and when the wind blows, a few of them drop onto the water.

Waist-deep in the river, an angler stands under the arching branches. Motionless as a stalking heron, he scans the water with observant eyes. So quiet is the angler that a deer thirty feet away browses unaware. Fifteen feet upstream from the angler, the dorsal fin of a large trout breaks the surface, leaves a zig-zag wake, then disappears. A few seconds later, at the same place, there is a subtle swirl, and the angler has a quick look at the nose of a feeding fish that has sucked down yet another hapless caddis.

The angler prepares to cast a size 14 Elk Hair Caddis. He makes one short cast slightly upstream from the feeding trout, and carefully manages the slack line as the fly drifts back down. There is a slow, confident swirl and his fly disappears. The hook is set, and the rod is swung to the side to lead the trout away from the trees and into open water. Line zips from the reel, and the trout leaps in brilliant sunshine.

When the trout is brought to the hand, the angler measures it. It is sixteen inches long, the best of the half-dozen fish he caught and released while working up this line of alder trees.

Deschutes River Trout

All trout in the Deschutes today are native wild fish. The typical trout hooked by anglers is between 10 and 15 inches long, although it is not uncommon to hook fish of 16 to 18 inches, and sometimes larger. Deschutes rainbows have distinctive coloring which has given them the nickname "redsides."

Deschutes River trout are active, acrobatic fish. They jump often, will make long runs, and do not tire easily. Anglers coming to the river for the first time should be prepared for strong, hard running fish.

The upper part of the river holds the most trout, probably because of the cooler water from Pelton Dam, a gentler river gradient that allows food to accumulate, and better spawning habitat. The population is slightly lower in the Maupin area (about two-thirds as many), and even lower below Sherars Falls (about one-fourth as many). The low trout population in the lower river is probably due to warmer water and poor spawning habitat.

Deschutes River trout are real home-bodies. Most fish stay within the same one mile stretch of river most of their life. Their principal diet is stoneflies, mayflies, and caddisflies, although they sometimes take midges, baby whitefish, snails, and an occasional crawfish.

Redsides become sexually mature in three to four years, when they are 11-13 inches in length. An individual trout spawns every two or three years after maturity, and lives approximately seven years in all. After maturity, the fish grow more slowly—only one-half inch to one inch per year.

Few anglers understand how hard spawning is on a trout. The bodily changes they go through are extreme, and it can take a couple of years for a spawned trout to totally regain its healthy condition. The first few weeks after spawning are the most crucial. During this period—typically April through mid-June—anglers should be especially careful with dark, lethargic trout. If you hook one, the best thing you can do (for your future and the trout's) is to break it off, rather than play it to exhaustion.

Another thing anglers can do is stay off the spawning areas (called "redds") during April to July. Spawning redds have fine gravel, less than one inch in diameter, and sometimes can be recognized by noting that vegetation has been scraped off some of the gravel. In spring, you can often see spawning fish on the redds. Just leave them alone, and seek other water. Your present and future sport will both be better.

Wild Trout. In 1979 ODFW ceased planting hatchery trout in the Deschutes, choosing instead to implement regulations that favored rebuilding the stock of wild trout. Since then, ODFW has implemented a "slot limit" so that only two trout longer than 10 inches or shorter than 13

All Deschutes River rainbows are wild trout. (Randy Stetzer photo)

inches could be kept. All other trout must be released unharmed.

The reason for this policy is that trout over 13 inches are the primary spawners, and the slot limit allows these big, hearty fish to perpetuate their superior genetic qualities.

The Deschutes River is one of the finest trout fisheries in North America. Without the regulations that support wild trout, fishing on the Deschutes would be like going to a stock pond with nice scenery. To perpetuate quality fishing like this, those who love the fish and the river need to follow the regulations, be careful when releasing wild fish (see Chapter 7), and support organizations that promote the conservation of wild fish.

Where to Fish

Outside of the spawning season, trout have two simple concerns: food, and a risk-free life with no hard work. This means you will find trout either in safe resting places, or where there is food, or where they get both in one place, or—most commonly—in safe resting places adjacent to or downstream from a source of food.

Common resting places and places with food are listed below. Following this, I suggest a simple procedure for locating trout, and describe six prime places to look for them in the Deschutes. Since at least

90 percent of trout fishing on the Deschutes is done with flies, this chapter is oriented toward fly fishing. Fishing with spinners in particular is discussed at the end of the chapter, but spin anglers will benefit from information contained in the fly fishing section.

Resting Places for Trout. In the Deschutes, the most common resting places are:
> Downstream or upstream from an obstruction such as a boulder
> In deep water
> Near the bottom
> In depressions, troughs, or drop-offs
> In quiet, slow moving water, often near the bank and under overhanging trees or grass

Food Producing and Collecting Places. The primary food production places in the Deschutes are:
> Riffles
> Weedbeds
> Long runs with rocky bottoms

You need to recognize where food is produced in the Deschutes so you can look for a downstream area where it is *collected*. This is important because trout in rivers do most of their feeding where food is collected, rather than where it is produced. The primary collecting areas are:
> Backeddies
> Current seams
> Current tongues
> Bank areas with overhanging trees or other vegetation.

Finding the Trout. Once you can recognize food producing and collecting places, you are ready to find the trout. Identifying the likely places to find trout is the most important thing an angler can do, yet most people skip this step. When they get to the river, they are as patient and subtle as a rutting moose. They wade quickly into the water and start casting away in the belief that if a trout takes their fly, they have found fish. Restrain yourself. Stop and take 60 seconds (or more) to look at the water and think. Follow the simple procedure below:

First, look for rising trout. OK, now you know where some fish are. But they might not be the best fish, or the easiest to catch, so don't stop here! Keep on with the rest of the steps below.

> *"Many anglers don't take the time to learn the basics of reading water to find out where trout commonly feed. These anglers can often be found standing in water where fish like to feed . . . and happily (and unproductively) casting to where the fish aren't."* Mike McLucas.

Next, identify likely resting areas for trout. Look at the underwater structure—boulders, drop-offs, troughs, etc. Structure is easier to spot if you wear polarizing sunglasses. Height can also be a big advantage, and the Deschutes' steep banks can be handy.

Then identify food producing areas. Are there any riffles or weedbeds?

Now look for food collecting areas downstream from food producing areas. Are there backeddies, current seams (fast water next to slow), overhanging trees, etc.?

Finally, are there resting places next to or combined with food collecting areas? If so, this is where you want to fish.

Six Prime Places to Fish in the Deschutes

This section does not describe specific places on the river, but *types* of water to fish. On any given day, only one or two of the water types described here may be productive. Each day, your primary job as an angler is to determine which type of water has responsive fish in it, and which tactics work best in that water. If you are having trouble finding receptive trout, try different tactics in each type of water until you hit the right combination. Then look for similar water, and fish it with the same tactics. Be aware that the situation can change during the day, as well as from one day to the next, so you need to be alert and flexible.

The Deschutes can be a moody river. One day you might be red hot fishing current seams with stonefly nymphs. Three days later you might return to the river and fish the same water with the same flies and tactics, and get skunked. If you stubbornly insist on fishing that same, unproductive water all day, your skunking is well deserved. With a little extra effort you might check out the backeddies and find the trout taking *Baetis* emergers, or adult caddis under the trees, or midge pupae in the seams at dusk.

The six types of productive fishing water discussed below are not the only places to fish, nor are the tactics described the only tactics that might work in that water. Anglers need to be aware of what works most of the time, and should use that as a basis to start fishing. However, you also need to be alert to when your bread-and-butter tactics are no longer appropriate and need to be changed.

The section following this one describes fly fishing tactics appropriate for these prime waters.

Current Seams. A current seam is a place where slow water is flowing next to fast water. Most often, seams are created when an obstruction, such as a rock or an island, causes the current to compress into a narrow "fast lane." The same forces that caused the current to gather into a narrow zone have collected insects and other trout food. Trout are no dummies. They sit in the quiet water next to the seam, or on the bottom under the seam, and wait for food to drift by. It's like sitting at a table in a Chinese dim sum restaurant while a waiter comes by with delicacies on a cart. You see something you like and nail it when it comes past you.

When fishing this kind of water with dry flies, cast into the faster water of the seam, as well as the slower water next to the seam. However, when fishing deep nymphs, place your fly in the slower water next to the fast water. The reason for this difference is that the nymph needs to be near the bottom, and the faster water usually prevents this from happening.

Drop-offs and Breaks. A drop-off is a place where the water gets suddenly deeper. There are many places like this in the Deschutes. Sometimes they are parallel to the current, as when it gets deep quickly as you wade towards mid-river. Other times the drop-off is perpendicular to the current, so that as you wade downstream it gets deeper.

A "break" is a special case where a drop-off follows a shallow riffle. Since the riffle is a food production zone, and the drop-off is a safety zone, breaks are prime areas in which to find trout.

You will often find small troughs and depressions in the bottom. Trout rest in these as well.

There are four good ways to locate a drop-off or break.

Color. One of the best clues is water color. The shallow water is brown, and the deeper water is green.

The water looks "restless." A lot of little waves are bouncing up and down but not going anywhere. This shows a place where fast water is

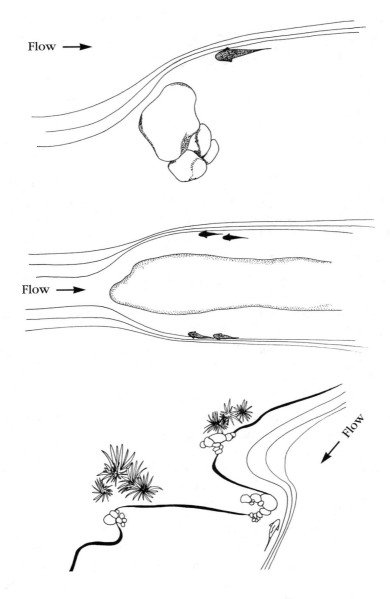

Three examples of current seams. Top—Rock compresses current. Middle—Island forms seams on both sides. Bottom—River flow is diverted and compressed by a point of land or a pile of boulders. In each example, trout lie in slower water and look for food that has been collected into a narrow zone by the current.

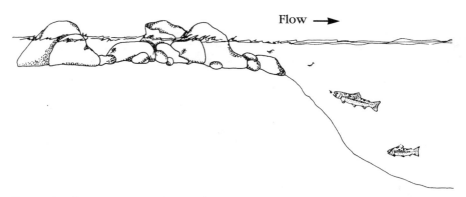

Flow ⟶

Example of a break—a drop-off after a riffle. Food is produced in the riffle, then washed into the flow. Trout rest in the relative safety of deeper, quieter water and pick off drifting insects.

meeting slow, and usually means there is a drop-off or break.

You see a riffle, but the water just downstream from it is moving slowly.

You feel it as you wade. In this case, you just blundered through the prime fishing zone. Oh well, remember the place for your next trip.

Sometimes breaks will have current tongues. These are shaped like the letter "V," with the point downstream. Current—and therefore drifting food—concentrates in the V. Cast your fly into the V and let it drift downstream. Trout will usually take your fly on the edge of the V.

When fishing breaks and drop-offs, start well below them and work your way upstream. At the end, you should be casting above the break and letting your fly drift over it into the quieter water.

Many people only fish this kind of water with nymphs, however it can offer excellent dry fly fishing as well.

Backeddies. Backeddies are places where the current doubles back on itself and revolves in a large circle. Anything drifting downstream, from a *Baetis* to a Buick, will get sucked into the backeddy if it comes anywhere near its current. Backeddies can offer the most demanding—and most rewarding—fishing on the Deschutes. Some of the biggest trout in the river will wait in the backeddy for food to come to them on an aquatic lazy susan.

Unfortunately, the prime places for fish are often the toughest places for fishing. On one hand, the outside edge of the backeddy usually has many micro-whirlpools that catch your fly and make it drag unnaturally. Trout will almost always reject your fly when this happens. Another problem with fishing the outside of a backeddy is that you are often casting across water that is moving in the opposite direction from the water where your fly lands. This creates drag almost instantly. Sometimes this part of a backeddy can be fished effectively if you use a slack cast. The slack cast is made by wiggling the rod as the cast is released, so the line lands in "S" curves; this lets the current pull the slack out of the line and delays the effects of drag.

On the other hand, the area next to the bank usually has the smoothest current, which makes the presentation easier. But trout near the bank are more wary because they are closer to potential predators (like anglers). In this case, cast so that your line does not pass over them. Also, hide yourself as much as possible, either by kneeling down or by getting behind a bush. By the end of the summer, these fish have been cast over so much that they head for the bottom at the first sign of an angler.

Banks and Overhangs. The Deschutes abounds in stoneflies, caddisflies, alder trees, and grass. These combine to provide outstanding fishing next to the riverbank. Stoneflies and caddis gather in the trees and other vegetation. As the day warms, they become more active. Trout wait in quiet water under, or downstream from, overhanging trees. They also lie next to grassy banks, using the overhanging grass for cover. In

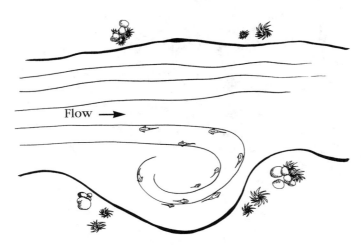

Trout wait for trapped insects to come to them on the aquatic "lazy susan" of a backeddy.

both types of bank water, trout gobble hapless bugs that blunder into the river. This gives the fly fisher hours of productive dry fly fishing, all of which is unrelated to hatch activity and which can continue for weeks after the last major stonefly or caddis hatch.

Prime bank fishing can be found where there is a shady spot sheltered by trees or grass, and the water is two to six feet deep and has a moderate current. If there are many large boulders on the bottom, so much the better. Watch carefully for feeding trout. Often all you will see is a quiet sip, or a dorsal fin that breaks the surface. You won't see these fish if you are drifting by in a boat or walking down the bank, so pick good looking water and start fishing it. You will usually be rewarded. You may need to carefully stalk each trout, so be stealthy. And yes, sometimes (frequently?) your fly and leader will become tangled in the

Bankside trees and grass are gathering places for insects, especially caddis and stoneflies. The overhead cover gives protection to trout, and drops insects into the river where waiting trout quietly sip them.

> *"The Deschutes is a big river, and newcomers are sometimes intimidated by its size. 'My gosh,' they think, 'there's so much water! The trout could be anywhere. I can't even cast half way across the river.' The thing to do is to divide the river into thirds, then concentrate on the third that is closest to you. Think of that third of a river as a small river, and look for places that trout might be in it."* John Smeraglio, river guide and owner of the Deschutes Canyon Fly Shop.

overhanging trees. Be philosophical, keep your cool, and don't spook the fish.

Boulder fields. Boulder fields offer trout a safe resting place because the boulders break the flow of the current and give good hiding places from predators. The boulders also tend to concentrate the current into narrow seams that trap food. Boulder fields are good places for stonefly nymphs to live, and Deschutes trout love stonefly nymphs. An ideal run has numerous large rocks, submerged or otherwise, moderate current, and is two to five feet deep.

Nymph fishing in boulder fields can be excellent, if sometimes frustrating. The frustrations come from hanging your fly on the boulders. Persist. There are good fish here, and if it was too easy it wouldn't be fun, right?

When fishing boulder fields with a deep nymph, fish all the water you can. However, when fishing dry flies and emergers, try to find foam lines and concentrate your fishing there. A foam line is a line of foamy bubbles. At first glance they may look like they occur at random, but in fact there are current forces that concentrate the foam into narrow channels. The same current that gathered the surface foam into a narrow line has also gathered surface food.

Flats. Flats are areas of smooth, moderately flowing current, with few visible obstructions. Flats can be good producers of certain kinds of insects, and trout will often rest in flats, seeking the safety of depth and mid-river.

It is the nature of flats that trout in them are usually scattered, and in a big river like the Deschutes that means they might as well be on the

Boulder fields offer prime habitat for large nymphs like stoneflies. Here trout find the best of all worlds: hiding places behind rocks, a break from the current, and food to eat.

moon. Therefore, they are tough to fish well with a fly unless there is a hatch in progress. Then, as trout rise to the surface, they reveal themselves and you know where to cast.

Because the best fishing in flats is during a hatch, you will be casting emergers and dry flies with an upstream presentation to sighted fish. When you see a rise, cast so your fly lands about four feet above where you saw the rise.

Presentation Tactics

Four presentation tactics are described below. Naturally, these are not the only methods that will hook trout in the Deschutes. However, most fly anglers will spend at least 80 percent of their time with these tactics.

In all cases, it is important to maintain close contact with your fly. This means minimizing the slack line between you and the fly. With a tight line you'll be able to strike quickly enough to hook trout. On an upstream cast, you need to pull in the slack as the fly and line drift down to you. Be careful not to disturb the fly as you do this. The objective is to have enough slack to avoid pulling the fly unnaturally, yet keep the line tight enough to allow a quick strike. Keep the index finger of your rod hand on the line, then pull in slack from behind it, as shown in the illustration.

Fishing the Deep Nymph. The biggest challenge in fishing a nymph on the bottom is getting the nymph *on the bottom*. Three good ways to do this are:

Use a weighted fly. Cast far enough upstream so the fly has time to sink to the bottom before it reaches the fish.

Put a removable split shot or other lead on the leader about 12-18 inches in front of the fly. Always use removable lead, such as split shot with wings, flat twist-on strips, or soft lead.

Put a small fly on a dropper with a heavily weighted fly, such as a stonefly nymph, on the point.

Regardless of which of these three methods you employ, use a floating line. Put a strike indicator—such as a small corkie or foam strip—on your leader six to eight feet above the fly (don't throw used strike indicators in the river!). Cast upstream. Ideally the fly and indicator should be in a straight line, parallel with the current. This produces a more natural drift of the nymph and helps the indicator work better.

As soon as the indicator sinks, jerks, moves sideways, or commits any other unnatural act, pull your rod downstream hard, maybe even hauling in line with your free hand. There is always more slack than you realize, so you have to move a lot of line to set the hook. With this presentation, you should avoid casting more than thirty feet of line. Beyond that distance you cannot detect the subtle movement of the indicator that announces a strike.

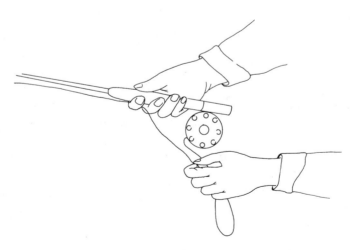

Pull line from behind the index finger of your rod hand.

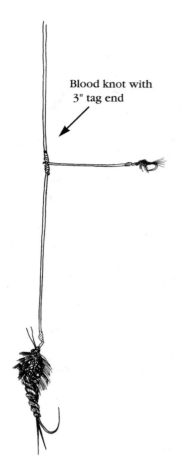

Blood knot with 3" tag end

Dropper rig. Put a heavy fly on the point, and a small fly on the dropper. Then you can get the small fly down deep. Trout may take either fly.

If the water is slow or very deep, your fly may sink the indicator after it has drifted for a while. If the indicator is sinking, move it up the leader, lengthening the leader if necessary. If it continues to sink, make more casts, but make them shorter so the fly does not drift as long on each cast.

A heavily weighted fly like a stonefly nymph can be a struggle to cast. You don't cast this rock like you would a size 16 dry fly. Let the fly, leader, and line hang in a straight line below you in the current. Then lift the rod so most of the line breaks free of the water; the fly will still be in the water, but will be near the surface. Pause briefly, then cast forward. The rod should travel in a wide, slow, convex arc. Bring the rod tip right down to the water, pointing straight at where you want the cast to go. If you have a problem with accuracy, you are probably casting too fast; this makes the fly line shock against the rod and bounce the fly in a different direction.

Presenting an Emerger Upstream. The word "emerger" refers loosely to any aquatic insect making the transition from an immature stage to an adult stage. Stoneflies are not available to trout at emergence, so only mayflies, midges, and caddis are fished this way. For a discussion of how each of these insects emerges, see the section on insects in this chapter.

There are two primary emerger presentations you need for fishing the Deschutes. The upstream emerger described here, and the caddis swing, described in the next section.

The upstream emerger tactic uses a floating line. Cast and present

Lob cast (also known as "chuck and duck"). With fly and line hanging below you in the current (1), lift rod to free line from water (2), pause briefly, then bring rod over in a wide arc (3).

the fly as you would a dry fly, except your fly is in the top few inches of water, not on the surface. Be careful with your strikes. Most anglers strike too often when fishing an emerger. They see a swirl near where they think their fly is and strike, ripping the line and leader through the water. Usually the trout took a real insect near their fly and there is no hookup, but the angler's strike disturbs the water and frightens the trout.

Downstream Caddis Pupa. Use a floating line. Cast straight across the river in slow water, or at more of an angle downstream (up to 60 degrees) in faster water. Mend line upstream or downstream so that the fly moves across the river at the same speed as the current moves down the river. Thus, your fly moves across the river at about a 45-degree angle. Let the fly swing across until it is directly below you, then let it hang there for a few seconds before casting again. Don't strike! Trout will usually hook themselves with this presentation. Start by casting a short line, then lengthen it a few feet with each additional cast. When you reach the limit of your casting, keep casting the same length of line but take a step downstream after you are done with each cast.

Presenting a Dry Fly Upstream. Use a floating line. Cast upstream—either directly above you or more across the river. As the fly comes back to you, pull in loose line so you can tighten quickly on the trout when it takes your fly. When pulling in line, be careful not to move the fly. Face your body in the direction in which you are casting: if you are casting straight upstream, face upstream; if you are casting across stream, face the direction your fly will land. Watch your fly. If it disappears in a swirl, raise your rod tip and tighten your fly line.

Fly Patterns

Deschutes trout are not as finicky about fly patterns as are trout in some rivers. They are, however, very sensitive to presentation, and your fly must be chosen so that it can be presented well.

The flies listed here are not the only effective patterns on the Deschutes. However, they are typical of what is often used, are available commercially, and are known to work well. The next section discusses the insects that are imitated by these flies, and the section after that is a chart which shows the patterns you will most likely need in each month of the year. The chart indicates correct color and size choices, as well as places to fish and presentations to use.

Dry Patterns

Mayfly—Parachute Blue Winged Olive (BWO); Thorax Pale Morning Dun (PMD); Mahogany Thorax Dun; PMD Spinner

Caddis—Elk Hair Caddis; Slow Water Caddis

Stonefly—Madam X; MacSalmon; Stimulator

Generic—Adams; Parachute Adams

Emerger Patterns

Mayfly—Floating Nymph BWO; Floating Nymph PMD

Midge—CDC Hatching Midge

Generic—Soft Hackle; Timberline Emerger

Pupa Patterns

Caddis—Sparkle Pupa

Midge—Suspender Pupa

Generic—Soft Hackle

Nymph/Larva Patterns

Mayfly/Generic—Hare's Ear; Flashback Pheasant Tail; Prince; Zug Bug; Serendipity

Caddis—Green Rock Worm; Randall's Caddis Larva; Cased Caddis

Stonefly—Kaufmann's Stone; Rubber Legs (black legs, red head); Matt's Fur

Other Patterns

Ovipositing Caddis—Diving Caddis

Terrestials—Dave's Hopper; MacHopper; CDC Ant

Slow Water Caddis

Elk Hair Caddis

Parachute BWO Thorax PMD PMD spinner Adams
(top view)

Dave's Hopper MacHopper

Stimulator Madam X Mac Salmon
(top view) (top view)

Deschutes River dry flies

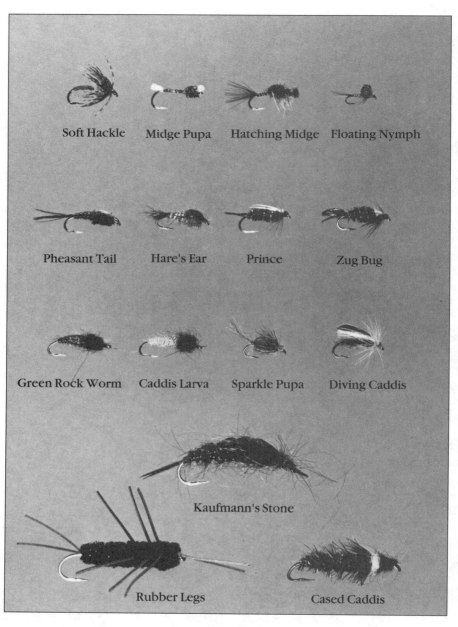

Deschutes River wet flies

Deschutes River Insects

The Deschutes River is rich in insect life, which is one reason it can support a blue ribbon trout fishery as well as large numbers of steelhead and salmon. This rich insect life has both quantity and diversity. Most days during the summer there will be hatches of two or three kinds of mayflies, midges of several flavors, craneflies, and heaven knows how many species of caddis. Besides all the hatching insects and active adults, there is another world of immature insects—nymphs, larvae, and pupae—living out the underwater stage of their lives.

You may recall that biology divides living creatures into categories. Insects are a class. The class called insects is sub-divided into different orders, which are further sub-divided into genera (the plural of genus), which are sub-divided into species ("species" is both a singular and plural word). The four most important insect orders on the Deschutes are: mayflies, caddisflies, stoneflies, and midges/craneflies.

Imitating the appearance and behavior of these insect orders is the essence of fly fishing. Since insect species can differ in behavior—as well as appearance—from one another, some knowledge of how they act is vital to successful angling in the Deschutes. Therefore, each insect order is discussed in general terms below. Guidelines for rudimentary identification of important Deschutes River insects is included.

Trout focus their feeding at those points in an insect's life when it is easiest to catch—at the insect's points of maximum vulnerability. These points of vulnerability depend on the insect's underwater habits and habitat, its methods of emerging into adulthood, and its habits as an adult. The points of vulnerability are usually predictable, and are different for each insect order. (They often vary within the order, as well.) An understanding of the differences in insect vulnerability will help you choose the correct fishing strategy. If your experience is primarily on streams where mayflies are the dominant aquatic insect, you should pay careful attention to the sections on stoneflies, caddisflies, and midges, since these common Deschutes River orders are vulnerable to trout in different ways than mayflies.

Mayflies. Mayflies live underwater as nymphs. When it is mature, a nymph comes out of the water and a winged adult emerges from the nymph's skin. The principal mayfly species that live in the Deschutes emerge in open water: the nymph rises to the surface of the water, its external skeleton splits open, and an adult comes out. This adult is called

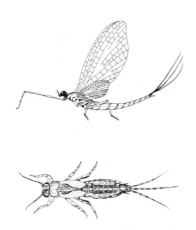

Typical Deschutes mayfly adult (top) and nymph (bottom).

a dun. Duns drift on the surface of the water for a brief space of time while their wings become ready for use, then they fly off. Within a day or two, the dun sheds its skin one more time and becomes a sexually mature spinner. Spinners mate, and the females return to the water to lay eggs. Often the spinners fall or remain exhausted on the surface of the water after laying their eggs.

Mayflies are particularly vulnerable to trout at several points in their life cycle. When they are nymphs, they may be washed into the current near the river bottom and devoured by waiting trout. This is particularly true a few weeks before they hatch, because they are more active and thus more exposed to the force of the current. Immediately prior to a hatch—for one or two hours—the nymphs are very active and are even more likely to be dislodged. This means that fishing nymphs in the weeks prior to an expected hatch, and particularly a few hours before the hatch starts, can be a good strategy.

As hatching nymphs rise to the surface, they might be picked off by trout, but they are most vulnerable when they reach the underside of the water's surface. There they hesitate briefly and are often taken by trout in the top few inches of water. This point of vulnerability is imitated by an emerger fly pattern and tactic.

As it emerges into a dun that drifts on the surface, an insect is again vulnerable to trout, and dry flies are a good strategy.

The spinners that return to the water and sprawl near death on its surface are also eaten by trout. Spinner patterns can be effective, but massive spinner falls on the Deschutes are rare enough that most anglers should not be concerned with them.

The principal mayflies encountered on the Deschutes are the Blue Winged Olive (*Baetis;* pronounced "Bee'-tis") which is the main cold weather hatcher; the Pale Morning Dun (*Ephemerella inermis*), which is the harbinger of summer warmth; and the Slate Winged Mahogany Dun (*Paraleptophlebia*), which makes sporadic appearances in September. Of these, *Baetis* is the most common. If there is one mayfly hatch you

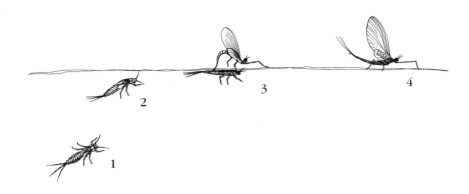

Emergence process for most Deschutes River mayflies. Nymph rises to surface (1), hesitates briefly under the surface (2), dun crawls out of nymph shuck (3), and dun drifts on surface waiting for its wings to be ready for flight (4). Different flies and tactics are needed to imitate each of these points of vulnerability.

should know how to fish on the Deschutes, it's the ubiquitous *Baetis*.

Stoneflies. Stoneflies come in many sizes, but the two largest species in the Deschutes are the salmonfly (*Pteronarcys californica*) and the golden stonefly (*Hesperoperla pacifica*). As nymphs, these mega-insects crawl around in the spaces between large rocks. They live mostly in or near riffled water because they need lots of oxygen. Because they live in fast riffles, they are often dislodged and drift helplessly in the current until they touch bottom again . . . or are eaten by waiting trout. Trout often wait downstream from riffles so they can pick off drifting stonefly nymphs.

The large stonefly nymphs live underwater for three years, when they reach maturity. Then—in May and June—they crawl along the bottom to shore, often getting dislodged (and eaten) in the process. Those that survive crawl out of the water and onto objects like trees branches and grass stems. Their skin (skeleton, really) splits open, and a winged adult emerges.

Unlike mayflies, which live only for a day or two as adults, stonefly adults live for several weeks. They congregate in the grass and tree branches, mate, and often get blown out of the trees into the water. Once they land in the water, the ever present, ever hungry trout is there to gobble them up.

Female stonefly adults return to the water in late afternoon and evening to drop their eggs on the surface of the water. Here again they

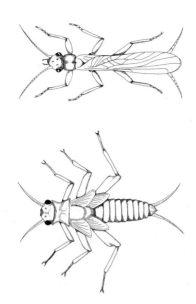

are vulnerable to trout.

Caddisflies. Caddisflies are one of the most diverse orders of aquatic insects in North America. There are over 1200 species (more than twice as many species as mayflies) that are adapted and specialized to a wide range of environments. The Deschutes is a caddis-rich river, hosting many species, but five genera are dominant and are discussed here.

Caddisflies mature in a different manner than mayflies and stoneflies. A caddisfly lives underwater as a larva—a kind worm with legs. The larvae (plural of larva; pronounced larvee) of some caddis species build

Stonefly adult (top) and nymph (bottom).

little cases out of pebbles or plant material and live in them until they become adults. Larvae of other caddis species live without cases.

As it nears maturity, each larva, regardless of species, builds a case, seals it up, and becomes a pupa. After a few weeks, the pupa cuts its way out of the case and makes its way to the open air—either by rising to the surface of the water, or by crawling to shore underwater. The adult caddis then emerges from the pupa and immediately flies off.

Caddis larvae that do not live in cases are especially vulnerable to being swept into the current and into a trout's mouth. Fishing imitations of these larvae can be productive, especially before an expected hatch.

The emergence of caddis is more complicated than that of other adult aquatic insects. Caddis have three primary methods of emergence, depending on the species:

Brief hesitation at surface. The pupa releases its grip on the bottom. It drifts briefly with the current next to the bottom, then rises quickly to the surface. The adult breaks out of the pupal skin and flies quickly away. Sometimes there is also a brief hesitation at the surface before the adult breaks out.

Swimming to shore. The pupa releases its grip on the bottom, drifts briefly next to the bottom, and rises to the surface—as described above.

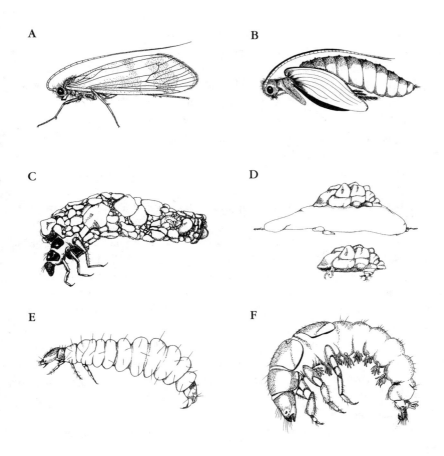

A

B

C

D

E

F

Caddis Gallery

A—Adult caddis.

B—Caddis pupa.

C—Tube case caddis larva. Typical of the Grannom (genus *Brachycentrus*) and October Caddis (genus *Dicosmoecus*).

D—Saddle case caddis larva. Typical of the Little Tan Short Horn Caddis (genus *Glossosoma*). The pebble case is stuck to the surface of rocks; larva is underneath it.

E—Free-living caddis larva. Typical of the Green Rock Worm (genus *Rhyacophila*).

F—Net-spinning caddis larva. Typical of the Spotted Caddis (genus *Hydropsyche*).

However, instead of the adult emerging, the pupa swims for the shore, climbs out onto rocks or grass, and the adult emerges there.

Crawling to shore. The pupa crawls to shore and emerges on rocks or grass. In the process of crawling for shore, many pupae are knocked loose into the current and are taken by trout.

To imitate the first case, use a caddis pupa, such as the Sparkle Pupa, on the bottom with the deep nymph presentation. You can also fish a pupa just subsurface with the emerger presentation.

For the second case, use a caddis pupa on the bottom, as above, or a caddis pupa just subsurface with the caddis swing presentation.

For the third case, your only option is to use a caddis pupa on the bottom.

How do you know which of the above situations is occurring? It's tricky. Look carefully at the water. If you are in a caddis hatch and see trout making subsurface rises, it's probably the first case. If you see caddis pupae just subsurface and moving across the current to shore, you are into the second case. The third case won't look like anything because the action is all on the bottom.

Of course, the one presentation that works all the time is a pupa presented on the bottom. During caddis season you can catch a lot of fish by using a dropper rig with a stonefly nymph on the point and a caddis pupa on the dropper.

Like stoneflies, adult caddis live several weeks. They hang around the shoreside trees and grass, eventually mate, and the females return to lay eggs. Some females drop their eggs into the water, while others actually dive below the surface, swim to the bottom, and lay their eggs.

Adult caddis are always dropping out of trees or grass and into the water. Fishing dry flies under trees and next to grassy banks is therefore a good strategy during caddis season. When females return to lay eggs, look carefully to see what they are doing. If they are dipping to the surface, then rising up again, fish a dry fly. But if they hit the surface and disappear, use a Diving Caddis imitation and the caddis swing tactic.

Midges and Craneflies. Midges and craneflies belong to insect order Diptera, or two-winged flies. Their cousins are the mosquito and the house fly. Midges and craneflies live underwater as larvae and then turn into pupae, much like caddisflies except they do not build cases. Pupae rise to the surface in open water, and the adult immediately emerges.

Because the larvae and pupae spend most of their lives in the silt of the river bottom, they are not vulnerable to trout until the pupae rise to the surface of the water. Most midges are very small, and it is hard for a midge pupa to break through the barrier of surface tension at the water's surface. They hang suspended and vulnerable just below the surface, and that is when trout eat them. Because they are drifting helplessly in the current, the suspended pupae are gathered into food collecting areas like current seams and backeddies, and this is where you will catch the most fish with midge imitations.

Insect Activity by Month

The aquatic insect life of the Deschutes is complex. In any one month, no single species can claim the trout's attention to the exclusion of all others. Trout shift the focus of their feeding throughout the day, and from one day to the next.

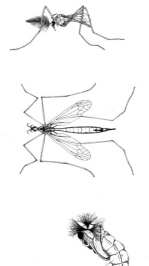

Midge adult (top), Cranefly adult (middle), Midge Pupa (bottom).

The charts offered here list the primary activity in each month, but anglers should be observant of what is happening in the river and never take anything for granted. Carry a nymph net, and examine both adult and underwater life to see what is active in the river. When in doubt, match the order, stage, size, and color of the insects you have collected.

The insect stage identified as "Ovi. Adult" on the charts is an ovipositing (egg-laying) adult.

> *"Deschutes River insect hatches are as varied and challenging as any trout stream, with intense hatches, masking hatches, a nd multiple hatches. Therefore, fly anglers must stay alert and be willing to change tactics frequently."*
> Rick Hafele, co-author of *Western Hatches.*

January

Stage	Pattern	Size	Colors	Where	Presentation	Comments
Blue winged olive (mayfly) *Baetis spp.*						
Nymph	Hare's Ear	16-18	Dark brown	Flats	Deep nymph	
Emerger	Floating Nymph; Soft Hackle	16-18	Dark brown	Flats; backeddies	Upstream emerger	
Dun	Thorax Dun	16-18	Olive body, blue dun wing	Flats; backeddies	Upstream dry	Hatches around 2 PM
Salmonfly; stonefly *Pteronarcys californica*						
Nymph	Kaufmann's Stone; Rubber Legs	8-10 (3X)	Black; dark brown	Seams; drop-offs; boulder fields	Deep nymph	
Golden stonefly *Hesperoperla pacifica*						
Nymph	Kaufmann's Stone; Rubber legs; Matts Fur	8-10 (3X)	Dark brown; tan	Seams; drop-offs; boulder fields	Deep nymph	
Spotted caddis (Net-spinning caddis) *Hydropsyche spp.*						
Larva	Randall's Caddis; Zugbug	12	Dark green	Breaks	Deep nymph	

February

Stage	Pattern	Size	Colors	Where	Presentation	Comments
	Blue winged olive (mayfly) *Baetis spp.*					
Nymph	Hare's Ear	16-18	Dark brown	Flats	Deep nymph	
Emerger	Floating Nymph; Soft Hackle	16-18	Dark brown	Flats; backeddies	Upstream emerger	
Dun	Thorax Dun	16-18	Olive body, blue dun wing	Flats; backeddies	Upstream dry	Hatches noon-3 PM
	Salmonfly; stonefly *Pteronarcys californica*					
Nymph	Kaufmann's Stone; Rubber Legs	8-10 (3X)	Black; dark brown	Seams; drop-offs; boulder fields	Deep nymph	
	Golden stonefly *Hesperoperla pacifica*					
Nymph	Kaufmann's Stone; Rubber legs; Matts Fur	8-10 (3X)	Dark brown; tan	Seams; drop-offs; boulder fields	Deep nymph	
	Spotted caddis (Net-spinning caddis) *Hydropsyche spp.*					
Larva	Randall's Caddis; Zugbug	12	Dark green	Breaks	Deep nymph	
	Midge Chironomidae family					
Pupa	Suspender Pupa; CDC Hatching Midge	16-20	Gray; olive	Seams; backeddies	Upstream emerger	Look for activity 9 AM-noon

March

Stage	Pattern	Size	Colors	Where	Presentation	Comments
Blue winged olive (mayfly) *Baetis spp.*						
Nymph	Hare's Ear	16-18	Dark brown	Flats	Deep nymph	
Emerger	Floating Nymph; Soft Hackle	16-18	Dark brown	Flats; backeddies	Upstream emerger	
Dun	Thorax Dun	16-18	Olive body, blue dun wing	Flats; backeddies	Upstream dry	Hatches noon-3 PM
Salmonfly; stonefly *Pteronarcys californica*						
Nymph	Kaufmann's Stone; Rubber Legs	8-10 (3X)	Black; dark brown	Seams; drop-offs; boulder fields	Deep nymph	
Golden stonefly *Hesperoperla pacifica*						
Nymph	Kaufmann's Stone; Rubber legs; Matts Fur	8-10 (3X)	Dark brown; tan	Seams; drop-offs; boulder fields	Deep nymph	
Spotted caddis (Net-spinning caddis) *Hydropsyche spp.*						
Larva	Randall's Caddis; Zugbug	12	Dark green	Breaks	Deep nymph	
Midge Chironomidae family						
Pupa	Suspender Pupa; CDC Hatching Midge	18	Gray; olive	Seams; backeddies	Upstream emerger	Look for activity 9 AM-noon

April

Stage	Pattern	Size	Colors	Where	Presentation	Comments
Blue winged olive (mayfly) *Baetis spp.*						
Nymph	Hare's Ear	16-18	Dark brown	Flats	Deep nymph	
Emerger	Floating Nymph; Soft Hackle	16-18	Dark brown	Flats, backeddies	Upstream emerger	
Dun	Thorax Dun	16-18	Olive body, blue dun wing	Flats, backeddies	Upstream dry	Hatches noon-3 PM
Salmonfly; stonefly *Pteronarcys californica*						
Nymph	Kaufmann's Stone; Rubber Legs	6-8 (3X)	Black; dark brown	Seams; drop-offs; boulder fields	Deep nymph	
Golden stonefly *Hesperoperla pacifica*						
Nymph	Kaufmann's Stone; Rubber legs; Matts Fur	8-10 (3X)	Dark brown; tan	Seams; drop-offs; boulder fields	Deep nymph	
Spotted caddis (Net-spinning caddis) *Hydropsyche spp.*						
Larva	Randall's Caddis; Zugbug	12	Dark green	Breaks	Deep nymph	
Grannom (Tube-case caddis) *Brachycentrus spp.*						
Pupa	Sparkle Pupa; Soft Hackle	16	Green body, tan shroud	Breaks	Deep nymph; Upstream emerger	Look for afternoon activity
Adult	Elk Hair Caddis	16	Dark brown body, tan wing	Banksides	Upstream dry	
Little tan short-horn caddis (Saddle-case caddis) *Glossosoma spp.*						
Pupa	Sparkle Pupa; Soft Hackle	18-20	Yellow body	Breaks	Deep Nymph; Caddis Swing	
Adult	Elk Hair Caddis	18-20	Tan bdy, drk wng	Bankside	Upstream dry	
Ovi. Adult	Diving Caddis	18-20	Tan bdy, drk wng	Flats	Caddis swing	
Green Rock Worm (Free-living caddis) *Rhyacophila spp.*						
Larva	Green Rock Worm	12-14	Green body,	Breaks	Deep nymph	

May

Stage	Pattern	Size	Colors	Where	Presentation	Comments
Salmonfly; stonefly *Pteronarcys californica*						
Nymph	Kaufmann's Stone; Rubber Legs	4-8 (3X)	Black; dark brown	Seams; drop-offs; boulder fields	Deep nymph	
Adult	MacSalmon; Madam X; Stimulator	6-8	Orange body	Seams; bankside	Upstream dry	Begins hatching mid-month; look for afternoon activity
Golden stonefly *Hesperoperla pacifica*						
Nymph	Kaufmann's Stone; Rubber legs; Matts Fur	6-8 (3X)	Dark brown; tan	Seams; drop-offs; boulder fields	Deep nymph	
Adult	MacSalmon; Madam X; Stimulator	8-10	Golden body	Seams; bankside	Upstream dry	When both golden stones and salmonflies are out, trout prefer goldens
Spotted caddis (Net-spinning caddis) *Hydropsyche spp.*						
Larva	Randall's Caddis; Zugbug	12	Dark green	Breaks	Deep nymph	
Grannom (Tube-case caddis) *Brachycentrus spp.*						
Pupa	Sparkle Pupa; Soft Hackle	16	Green body, tan shroud	Breaks	Deep nymph; Upstream emerger	Look for afternoon activity
Adult	Elk Hair Caddis	16	Dark brown body, tan wing	Banksides	Upstream dry	
Green Rock Worm (Free-living caddis) *Rhyacophila spp.*						
Larva	Green Rock Worm	12-14	Green body, black head	Breaks	Deep nymph	
Pupa	Sparkle Pupa	14	Green body	Breaks	Deep nymph; upstream emerger	Mid-afternoon hatches
Adult	Elk Hair Caddis	14	Dark olive body, gray wing	Bankside	Upstream dry	
Ovi. Adult	Diving Caddis	14	Gray wing over olive body	Mid-river	Caddis swing	

June

Stage	Pattern	Size	Colors	Where	Presentation	Comments
Pale morning dun (mayfly) *Ephemerella inermis*						
Nymph	Pheasant Tail; Hares Ear	14-16	Dark brown	Flats	Deep nymph	Afternoon or morning hatches
Adult	Thorax Dun	16-18	Pale yellow	Flats; backeddies	Upstream dry	
Salmonfly; stonefly *Pteronarcys californica*						
Nymph	Kaufmann's Stone; Rubber Legs	4-8 (3X)	Black; dark brown	Seams; drop-offs; boulder fields	Deep nymph	
Adult	MacSalmon; Madam X; Stimulator	6-8	Orange body	Seams; bankside	Upstream dry	Best in afternoon
Golden stonefly *Hesperoperla pacifica*						
Adult	MacSalmon; Madam X; Stimulator	8-10	Golden body	Seams; bankside	Upstream dry	When both golden stones and salmonflies are out, trout prefer goldens
Spotted caddis (Net-spinning caddis) *Hydropsyche spp.*						
Larva	Randall's Caddis; Zugbug	12	Dark green	Breaks	Deep nymph	
Pupa	Sparkle Pupa	14	Olive body, tan shroud	Breaks; flats	Deep nymph; upstream emerger	Afternoon, evening hatches
Adult	Elk Hair Caddis	14	Brown body, tan wing	Bankside	Upstream dry	
Ovi. Adult	Diving Caddis	14	Tan wing over brown body	Flats; riffles	Caddis swing	

July

Stage	Pattern	Size	Colors	Where	Presentation	Comments
Pale morning dun (mayfly) *Epbemerella inermis*						
Nymph	Pheasant Tail; Hares Ear	14-16	Dark brown	Flats	Deep nymph	Late afternoon or morning hatches on hot days; early afternoon on cool days
Adult	Thorax Dun	16-18	Pale yellow	Flats; backeddies	Upstream dry	
Blue winged olive (mayfly) *Baetis spp.*						
Nymph	Hare's Ear	18	Dark brown	Flats	Deep nymph	
Emerger	Floating Nymph; Soft Hackle	18	Dark brown	Flats, backeddies	Upstream emerger	
Dun	Thorax Dun	18	Olive body, blue dun wing	Flats, backeddies	Upstream dry	Hatches morning and evening
Spotted caddis (Net-spinning caddis) *Hydropsycbe spp.*						
Larva	Randall's Caddis; Zugbug	12	Dark green	Breaks	Deep nymph	
Pupa	Sparkle Pupa	14	Olive body, tan shroud	Breaks; flats	Deep nymph; upstream emerger	Afternoon, evening hatches
Adult	Elk Hair Caddis	14	Brown body, tan wing	Bankside	Upstream dry	
Ovi. Adult	Diving Caddis	14	Tan wing over brown body	Flats; riffles	Caddis swing	

August

Stage	Pattern	Size	Colors	Where	Presentation	Comments
Pale morning dun (mayfly) *Ephemerella inermis*						
Nymph	Pheasant Tail; Hares Ear	14-16	Dark brown	Flats	Deep nymph	Late afternoon or morning hatches on hot days; early afternoon on cool days
Adult	Thorax Dun	16-18	Pale yellow	Flats; backeddies	Upstream dry	
Blue winged olive (mayfly) *Baetis spp.*						
Nymph	Hare's Ear	18	Dark brown	Riffles	Deep nymph	
Emerger	Floating Nymph; Soft Hackle	18	Dark brown	Riffles, backeddies	Upstream emerger	
Dun	Thorax Dun	18	Olive body, blue dun wing	Below riffles; backeddies	Upstream dry	Hatches morning and evening
Spotted caddis (Net-spinning caddis) *Hydropsyche spp.*						
Larva	Randall's Caddis; Zugbug	12	Dark green	Breaks	Deep nymph	
Pupa	Sparkle Pupa	14	Olive body, tan shroud	Breaks; flats	Deep nymph; upstream emerger	Afternoon, evening hatches
Adult	Elk Hair Caddis	14	Brown body, tan wing	Bankside	Upstream dry	
Ovi. Adult	Diving Caddis	14	Tan wing over brown body	Flats; riffles	Caddis swing	
Little tan short-horn caddis (Saddle-case caddis) *Glossosoma spp.*						
Pupa	Sparkle Pupa; Soft Hackle	18-20	Yellow body	Breaks	Deep Nymph; caddis Swing	
Adult	Elk Hair Caddis	18-20	Tan bdy, dk wng	Bankside	Upstream dry	
Ovi. Adult	Diving Caddis	18-20	Tan bdy, dk wng	Flats	Caddis swing	
Green Rock Worm (Free-living caddis) *Rhyacophila spp.*						
Larva	Green Rock Worm	12-14	Green body, black head	Breaks	Deep nymph	

September

Stage	Pattern	Size	Colors	Where	Presentation	Comments
Blue winged olive (mayfly) *Baetis spp.*						
Nymph	Hare's Ear	18-20	Dark brown	Riffles	Deep nymph	
Emerger	Floating Nymph; Soft Hackle	18-20	Dark brown	Riffles; backeddies	Upstream emerger	
Dun	Thorax Dun	18-20	Olive body, blue dun wing	Below riffles; backeddies	Upstream dry	Hatches morning and evening
Slate-winged mahogany dun (mayfly) *Paraleptophlebia spp.*						
Emerger	Timberline Emerger	14-16	Dark brown	Slow water; backeddies	Upstream emerger	Hatches afternoon
Dun	Thorax Dun	14-16	Dark brown	Slow water; backeddies	Upstream dry	
Salmonfly; stonefly *Pteronarcys californica*						
Nymph	Kaufmann's Stone; Rubber Legs	8-10 (3X)	Black; dark brown	Seams; drop-offs; boulder fields	Deep nymph	
Golden stonefly *Hesperoperla pacifica*						
Nymph	Kaufmann's Stone; Rubber legs; Matts Fur	8-10 (3X)	Dark brown; tan	Seams; drop-offs; boulder fields	Deep nymph	
Little tan short-horn caddis (Saddle-case caddis) *Glossosoma spp.*						
Pupa	Sparkle Pupa; Soft Hackle	18-20	Yellow body	Breaks	Deep Nymph; Caddis Swing	
Adult	Elk Hair Caddis	18-20	Tan body, dark wing	Bankside	Upstream dry	
Ovi. Adult	Diving Caddis	18-20	Tan body, dark wing	Flats	Caddis swing	

September—continued

Green Rock Worm (Free-living caddis) *Rhyacophila spp.*

Stage	Fly	Size	Body	Location	Technique	Notes
Larva	Green Rock Worm	12-14	Green body, black head	Breaks	Deep nymph	Mid-afternoon hatches
Pupa	Sparkle Pupa	14	Green body	Breaks	Deep nymph; upstream emerger	
Adult	Elk Hair Caddis	14	Dark olive bdy, gray wing	Bankside	Upstream dry	
Ovi. Adult	Diving Caddis	14	Gray wing over olive body	Mid-river	Caddis swing	

October caddis (Tube-case caddis) *Dicosmoecus spp.*

Stage	Fly	Size	Body	Location	Technique	Notes
Adult	Stimulator	4	Orange body	Seams; bankside	Upstream dry	

Midge Chironomidae family

Stage	Fly	Size	Body	Location	Technique	Notes
Pupa	Suspender Pupa; CDC Hatching Midge	16-20	Gray; olive	Seams; backeddies	Upstream emerger	Look for activity 9 AM-noon

October

Stage	Pattern	Size	Colors	Where	Presentation	Comments
Blue winged olive (mayfly) *Baetis spp.*						
Nymph	Hare's Ear	18	Dark brown	Riffles	Deep nymph	
Emerger	Floating Nymph; Soft Hackle	18	Dark brown	Riffles; backeddies	Upstream emerger	
Dun	Thorax Dun	18	Olive body, blue dun wing	Below riffles; backeddies	Upstream dry	Hatches afternoon
Salmonfly; stonefly *Pteronarcys californica*						
Nymph	Kaufmann's Stone; Rubber Legs	8-10 (3X)	Black; dark brown	Seams; drop-offs; boulder fields	Deep nymph	
Golden stonefly *Hesperoperla pacifica*						
Nymph	Kaufmann's Stone; Rubber legs; Matts Fur	8-10 (3X)	Dark brown; tan	Seams; drop-offs; boulder fields	Deep nymph	
Little tan short-horn caddis (Saddle-case caddis) *Glossosoma spp.*						
Pupa	Sparkle Pupa; Soft Hackle	18-20	Yellow body	Breaks	Deep Nymph; Caddis Swing	
Adult	Elk Hair Caddis	18-20	Tan body, dark wing	Bankside	Upstream dry	
Ovi. Adult	Diving Caddis	18-20	Tan body, dark wing	Flats	Caddis swing	

Green Rock Worm (Free-living caddis) *Rhyacophila spp.*						
Larva	Green Rock Worm	12-14	Green body, black head	Breaks	Deep nymph	Mid-afternoon hatches
Pupa	Sparkle Pupa	14	Green body	Breaks	Deep nymph; upstream emerger	
Adult	Elk Hair Caddis	14	Dark olive body, gray wing	Bankside	Upstream dry	
Ovi. Adult	Diving Caddis	14	Gray wing over olive body	Mid-river	Caddis swing	
October caddis (Tube-case caddis) *Dicosmoecus spp.*						
Adult	Stimulator	4	Orange body	Seams; bankside	Upstream dry	
Midge	Chironomidae family					
Pupa	Suspender Pupa; CDC Hatching Midge	16-20	Gray; olive	Seams; backeddies	Upstream emerger	Look for activity 9:00-noon

November

Stage	Pattern	Size	Colors	Where	Presentation	Comments
Salmonfly; stonefly *Pteronarcys californica*						
Nymph	Kaufmann's Stone; Rubber Legs	8-10 (3X)	Black; dark brown	Seams; drop-offs; boulder fields	Deep nymph	
Golden stonefly *Hesperoperla pacifica*						
Nymph	Kaufmann's Stone; Rubber legs; Matts Fur	8-10 (3X)	Dark brown; tan	Seams; drop-offs; boulder fields	Deep nymph	
Green Rock Worm (Free-living caddis) *Rhyacophila spp.*						
Larva	Green Rock Worm	12-14	Green body, black head	Breaks	Deep nymph	
Pupa	Sparkle Pupa	14	Green body	Breaks	Deep nymph; upstream emerger	
Adult	Elk Hair Caddis	14	Dark olive body, gray wing	Bankside	Upstream dry	Afternoon, evening activity
Ovi. Adult	Diving Caddis	14	Gray wing over olive body	Mid-river	Caddis swing	
Spotted caddis (Net-spinning caddis) *Hydropsyche spp.*						
Larva	Randall's Caddis; Zugbug	12	Dark green	Breaks	Deep nymph	
Midge Chironomidae family						
Pupa	Suspender Pupa; CDC Hatching Midge	16-20	Gray; olive	Seams; backeddies	Upstream emerger	Look for activity late afternoon

December

Stage	Pattern	Size	Colors	Where	Presentation	Comments
Blue winged olive (mayfly) *Baetis spp.*						
Nymph	Hare's Ear	16-18	Dark brown	Flats	Deep nymph	
Emerger	Floating Nymph; Soft Hackle	16-18	Dark brown	Flats, backeddies	Upstream emerger	
Dun	Thorax Dun	16-18	Olive body, blue dun wing	Flats, backeddies	Upstream dry	Hatches around 2 PM
Salmonfly; stonefly *Pteronarcys californica*						
Nymph	Kaufmann's Stone; Rubber Legs	8-10 (3X)	Black; dark brown	Seams; drop-offs; boulder fields	Deep nymph	
Golden stonefly *Hesperoperla pacifica*						
Nymph	Kaufmann's Stone; Rubber legs; Matts Fur	8-10 (3X)	Dark brown; tan	Seams; drop-offs; boulder fields	Deep nymph	
Spotted caddis (Net-spinning caddis) *Hydropsyche spp.*						
Larva	Randall's Caddis; Zugbug	12	Dark green	Breaks	Deep nymph	
Midge Chironomidae family						
Pupa	Suspender Pupa; CDC Hatching Midge	16-20	Gray; olive	Seams; backeddies	Upstream emerger	Look for activity late afternoon

Fishing for Trout with Spinning Gear

Though spinning gear is not used for trout fishing on the Deschutes as much as fly fishing gear, it can be effective. Since fishing for trout with bait is illegal throughout the river, your choices are to use spinners or a casting bubble with a fly. Remember that all hooks must be barbless or have the barb pinched down flat.

Gear. A standard trout spinning rod with an open face reel is adequate for Deschutes trout. Some anglers prefer ultra-light gear, and it will work fine here if it is of good quality. Four to six pound line is strong enough for trout fishing.

Using Spinners. Standard small trout spinners such as Mepps, Panther Martin, and Rooster Tails all work here. You will also pick up whitefish on these lures, in fact possibly twice as many whitefish as trout. Bright spinners can be used all day in the Deschutes due to the off-color water.

The best places to cast are near rocks and on the flats. While it is generally not productive to fly fish a flat when there is no hatch, spinners can be effective because you cover more water and the spinner can attract fish from farther away. Retrieve the spinner at the slowest speed that makes the blade turn over and keeps the lure off the bottom. This will vary depending on the strength of the current where the spinner is. As the spinner drifts downstream from you, the current will spin the blade with very little effort on your part. On the other hand, when you are retrieving a spinner that is upstream or across the stream, you will need to reel faster to get the proper action.

When fishing the flats, begin casting at a 45-degree angle upstream. Successive casts should be a little more downstream. Space your casts so each new cast lands about three feet downstream from the previous cast.

When trout are rising to an active insect hatch, you are unlikely to catch many on spinners. The fish are focused on the insects and can rarely be tempted by anything else.

Using a Casting Bubble. A casting bubble lets you fish for trout in a manner similar to fly fishing. You can fish most of the prime fly fishing water (see above) using the same flies. In fact, if you are going to fish this way, you should be familiar with the entire section on fly fishing.

To fish dry flies and emergers, rig the casting bubble as shown below. With this rig it is important to have the fly between the bubble

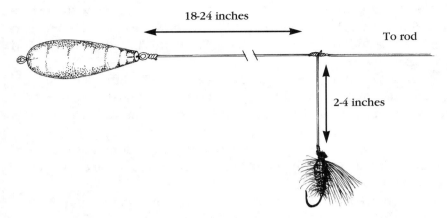

18-24 inches

To rod

2-4 inches

Rigging a casting bubble for a dry fly or emerger.

and the rod.

The only productive waters virtually off-limits to spin fishers, even with a casting bubble, are the stretches under the trees. It is just too easy to blow your cast with a spinning rod and hang your whole rig up in the branches. You will be better off to fish downstream from the trees, or just outside them.

Deschutes trout often take nymphs on the river bottom, particularly stonefly nymphs. Fishing nymphs with a spinning rod and casting bubble takes a little modification. The bubble must be between the rod and the fly, and you need a six to eight foot leader from the bubble to the fly. This rig is shown below.

This method of fishing is analogous to the "deep nymph" tactic described earlier in this chapter. It is effective with stonefly nymphs and other heavily weighted flies, or with small nymphs with some split shot on the leader. Once you are rigged up, pick suitable water—current seams, drop offs, boulder fields—and cast upstream. As your bubble drifts back to you, reel in line. Reel in fast enough to keep good contact with the bubble so you can strike quickly, but not so fast as to drag the

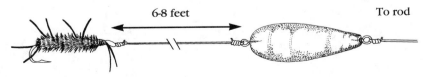

6-8 feet

To rod

Rigging a casting bubble for a deep nymph

bubble towards you. The bubble needs to float naturally with the current. Once the bubble is downstream, a belly will form in the line, and the bubble (and fly) will start to drag. When this happens, reel in and cast again.

You should only cast about 30 feet because it is difficult to tell what is happening with your bubble if you cast farther than this. Cast so as to cover the water upstream and in front of you. Then walk upstream 15 feet or so, and do it again.

When a trout takes your fly, the bubble will suddenly stop or submerge. Immediately swing your rod downstream, maybe even reeling in line as you do so.

Be sure to take lots of extra flies when you fish this way. You're bound to lose several on the rocks or in the trees during a day's fishing. Bring extra casting bubbles, too.

9

Fishing for Steelhead
and Salmon

In the half-light of early dawn, an angler wades into the Deschutes. He is familiar with the water he is about to fish. Every subtle change of current, every hidden rock, each trough where a steelhead might lie is known to him. He begins casting his fly short, using only 20 feet of line. With each cast a little more line goes out, and soon he is stepping methodically down the run, covering the water with graceful 70-foot casts and smooth presentations.

Across the river, an angler with different gear wades into water of a different nature. He begins casting a spinner into water that he, too, knows well. The two fishermen silently acknowledge each other's presence, aware that, though the water they are fishing and the tackle they are using may differ, there is much that unites them: a love of the river, an understanding of the fish they pursue, a dedication to "doing it right" and deserving each fish they hook.

Half an hour into his run, the fly angler feels a sharp pluck on his fly, but gets no hook up. He holds his position and casts again, identically to the previous cast. This time everything goes tight: the line straightens, the rod bends, the reel sings. A hundred feet away a prime wild steelhead breaks water. It hangs briefly in the air, glowing chrome-pink in the gathering dawn, then falls back into the river with a splash.

The spin fisherman, intuitively aware that something has happened, looks across to see the fly fisher's steelhead leap again. He pauses briefly to watch, then returns his attention to the water before him. He casts his spinner and retrieves it slowly, just fast enough to turn the blade over. There is a sudden grab, and for him, too, everything goes tight.

The two anglers glance at each other across the water, and each nods to the other in silent acknowledgment of their common bond.

Deschutes River Steelhead

Steelhead. Genetically, steelhead are nearly identical to rainbow trout, except steelhead have an urge to migrate to the ocean. Juvenile steelhead stay in the river until they are about 7 inches long. Then—in the spring—their body changes so they can survive in salt water, and they travel to the Pacific Ocean. There they feed and grow large, returning to the river in two or three years.

Deschutes River wild steelhead are typically 5-8 pounds when they return from the ocean. When hooked, they run fast, hard, and long. A good fish will give you sport to remember all winter. Deschutes steelhead are referred to as "summer run" steelhead because they begin arriving in mid-summer. Although some fish will arrive as late as December, they are still classed as "summer runs," regardless of how cold you get fishing for them.

Steelhead begin returning to the river in mid-July. By late September, they are well dispersed between Pelton Dam and the mouth of the river. As explained below, not all steelhead in the Deschutes are wild fish, nor are all the hatchery fish entering the Deschutes originally stocked here.

When steelhead first enter fresh water, they rarely feed. Some fish that have been in the river for a long time revert to their juvenile ways and start to feed a little.

After spawning in early spring, usually in the tributary creeks, many begin feeding regularly and quickly regain a healthy body condition. They are occasionally caught in the river in the spring as they migrate back to the ocean.

Steelhead Habits. When they migrate, steelhead travel four to six miles a day, usually in the top ten feet of water. They are apt to move during the dim light of dawn and dusk, and they may travel all night when the moon is full. However, steelhead do not migrate every day and sometimes hold in the same place for several days.

Steelhead are individualistic fish; they do not school-up like salmon. On the other hand, steelhead have a common preference for certain types of water: a particular current speed and depth, and sometimes boulders for protection and to break the flow. A long section of water that meets these preferences may hold many fish. The Wagonblast pool in the lower river is an example of such a staging area. Other, shorter sections of the river may satisfy a steelhead's preferences, but because they are shorter they hold fewer fish.

Wild Steelhead and Hatchery Steelhead. Hatchery steelhead have a tendency to keep traveling upriver without holding long in staging areas. This makes them less available to anglers than wild fish. It also means that hatchery fish—being less rested—sometimes do not fight as hard as wild fish. Also, hatchery fish do not seem to take flies and lures as readily as wild fish. Perhaps one reason for this is that hatchery steelhead are raised in concrete tanks in a "mob" environment and may not have the same kind of territorial urges as wild fish. For whatever reason, the hatchery steelhead are not as easily caught and are often not as much sport when they are hooked.

Hatchery steelhead have one purpose: meat. Don't feel bad about killing one and taking it home. Be aware, however, that fish taken when the water is warm (around 70 degrees, as it often is in the lower river in August and early September) have poor quality meat. The warm water tends to soften the flesh, and it loses flavor.

The fishing regulations call for the release of all wild steelhead. Hatchery fish have the adipose fin cut off when they are small. The adipose fin is the little one on the top of the fish, half way between the tail and the big dorsal fin. The cut is healed over when the fish returns to the river.

Wild Steelhead Management. Management of Deschutes wild steelhead is complicated by the presence of hatchery steelhead. Some of these hatchery fish were released into the Deschutes by ODFW, but many are from hatcheries elsewhere, like Idaho. In summer months the

"Sixty-one percent of the steelhead my clients have landed are wild fish. Yet wild fish are less than one-third of the steelhead in the river. This shows how important it is to sport fishers to take care of wild steelhead, both in enhancing their habitat and properly releasing them. Without the wild fish, your chances of hooking a steelhead in the Deschutes would decline drastically." Randy Stetzer, river guide and author of *Flies: The Best One Thousand.* Randy has kept detailed statistics on the hundreds of steelhead his clients have hooked and landed in the last 13 years.

Late season steelhead. (Randy Stetzer photo)

Columbia River warms, and steelhead bound for other rivers come into the Deschutes seeking cooler water. When they were juveniles, many of these fish were barged or trucked around the Columbia and Snake River dams so they could get to the ocean. Unfortunately, some of them weren't sufficiently "imprinted" with their home river, so once they stray into the Deschutes, they stay in the Deschutes rather than continue their migration.

Not all of these hatchery strays are caught and killed, and some remain to spawn with native Deschutes fish. Of the non-wild fish that remain in the river until spawning time, over one-third are strays from other hatcheries. Even if ODFW stocked no hatchery steelhead, there would be hatchery fish in the river, and some would spawn here.

Another factor that complicates management of wild steelhead is that most of the tributary creeks where they spawn are under private ownership. The riparian zones of some of these creeks are in poor shape due to years of unrestricted cattle grazing. This means that the spawning and rearing habitat for wild steelhead is degraded and diminished. Fisheries managers are working cooperatively with some area ranchers to improve habitat on tributary creeks.

Wild steelhead entering the river tend to stay in the lower part of the river longer. Through mid-September, the water temperature in this part of the river can be near 70 degrees. Under these conditions, it is essential to play fish quickly so they can recover quickly. Also, avoid handling wild fish any more than necessary. Don't touch them except to remove the hook, and don't use a net. Revive them carefully (see Chapter 7), and let them go on to perpetuate their species—and your sport.

Fishing for Steelhead with Flies

Gear. Most steelhead fly fishing tactics on the Deschutes require a nine or nine and one-half foot rod capable of casting 7 or 8 weight line. Most anglers use an 8 weight rod. Although a strong 6 weight rod is sometimes used and can do double duty casting for trout, it's a bit underpowered for steelhead fishing. Graphite rods are recommended because of their ability to punch through the strong up-river wind that develops most afternoons.

Use a reel with a good drag system, and keep it well lubricated. These fish can really run, and a "dry" reel can overheat and fall apart. For most summer-run techniques, a floating line is sufficient. Some anglers prefer a weight forward line so they can cast farther and cover more water. Others prefer a double taper line because it roll casts better, allowing them to fish runs where the bank is brushy. In either case, you should have 100 to 200 yards of backing.

Flies. There is no magic to choosing a steelhead fly pattern for the Deschutes. The fish are not fussy, and most standard patterns work equally well. Common choices are Skunk, Green Butt Skunk, Freight Train, Coal Car, Signal Light, Max Canyon, Muddler, and Street Walker.

If you are a good caster and have a strong rod, you might want to try a two-fly rig with a skating pattern on the dropper, as shown below.

Leaders. When the afternoon and evening wind comes whooshing up the canyon, casting can become a struggle. For good fishing, your leader and fly need to turn over when you cast, and the wind can make this difficult. Many commercial leaders "wimp out" on the Deschutes

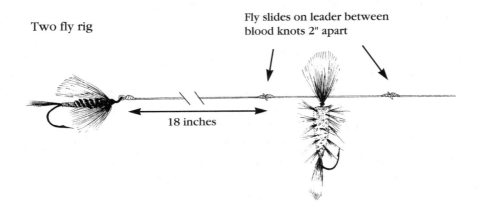

Two fly rig

Fly slides on leader between blood knots 2" apart

18 inches

when the wind starts because they don't have the stiffness and proportions to transfer power through the leader to the fly. This is why many Deschutes veterans tie up their own leaders. Here is a proven steelhead leader formula for the Deschutes. It is based on Maxima material and yields a 10 foot, 1X leader.

Diameter of Segment (inches)	Length of Segment (inches)
.024	28
.022	22
.020	8
.017	8
.015	8
.013	8
.012	10
.010	30

When fishing for steelhead, check your leader frequently for wind knots and abrasion. Replace weakened sections as soon as you notice them. When you may only hook one or two fish a day, you don't want to immediately lose them due to a weak leader.

Recognizing Good Steelhead Fly Fishing Water. The primary determinates of where a steelhead will rest are the speed of the current and the depth of the water. The classic Deschutes River steelhead fly fishing run is three to six feet deep with the current moving at about the speed of a walk. Underwater structures, such as ledges and rocks, can be important, but are not essential. They break the flow of current and provide shelter and rest for steelhead. Some good runs are so strewn with rubble that you can hardly wade.

Often, a good run follows a riffle formed by a point of land or a pile of boulders. The steelhead lie in the transition zone between the faster water formed by the riffle and the slower water near shore. Some steelhead runs are very long. For example, the Wagonblast run in the lower river is almost one mile in length.

The tailout of a run—where the bottom rises up in anticipation of the following riffle—can be very productive, too. However, fish in tailouts are more wary due to the shallow water, and the best time to fish them is in the low light of dawn or dusk.

Poor steelhead waters include places where a backeddy forms after

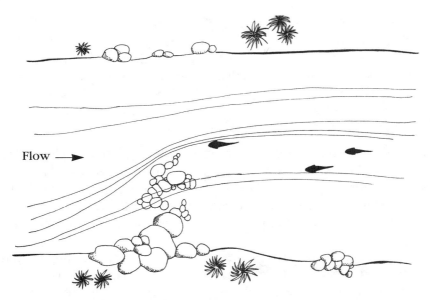

Typical steelhead run. Fish lie in quiet water following a riffle or point of land.

a riffle. Sudden transitions (where very fast water is next to slow water) are also unproductive.

Some beginning steelhead fly fishers believe that steelhead lie only at mid-river, in very deep water. These anglers wade out as far as they dare and cast at the limits of their ability (and frequently beyond). This is rarely necessary. Sometimes you have to wade deep to reach water of the right speed or structure, but usually you shouldn't have to wade much past your knees. Steelhead can be found in surprisingly shallow water. Many times there are slots of good water right up against the bank near overhanging trees.

Recognizing productive water is the biggest challenge to beginning steelheaders. Examine the waters you find steelheaders frequenting. You can only do this by fishing them. Check out the speed, depth, and underwater structure. Then branch out and seek water with similar characteristics.

Begin by developing your own list of "dirty dozen" good steelhead runs. Then each time you go fishing, try at least one new stretch of water instead of fishing the same old runs. Soon you will begin to recognize good steelhead water, and you will enjoy the special pleasure that comes from catching a steelhead in water you found on your own. After a while, you will have your own "top forty," and when the river is crowded, with people stacked up in the well-known runs, you will still have good water to go to.

It takes time and effort to find and learn productive steelhead water. You never know a run until you fish it, and often it takes several passes to learn a run well. But once you know a run, you have it in your permanent repertory because, given similar river conditions, steelhead will return to the same places year after year.

Steelhead Fly Fishing Tactics. I once met a fishing guide who claimed to know everything you can say with certainty about steelhead: "They're born in a river, they go to the ocean, and they come back to a river to spawn." That's it. Everything else you say may apply to most steelhead, to some steelhead, or to one or two steelhead. But never to all steelhead.

There are many different tactics that work to catch steelhead in the Deschutes. What is described here is the "Steelhead Classic" approach.

Cast across river at a 45-degree angle downstream. Mend line to keep the fly line as parallel with the current as possible, and moving slowly and steadily across the river. Usually an upstream mend is needed since this helps slow the drift of the fly. However, sometimes—especially at the beginning of a run—the current near the angler is slower, and a downstream mend is needed.

When you mend line, it helps if you throw extra line into the mend. This helps prevent the fly from being pulled closer to you. Saving a little extra line from your cast allows you to throw the mend as soon as possible after your cast.

As your fly swings across the current, follow the fly with your rod. Don't do anything else! Don't wiggle your rod, mend line again, strip line in, etc. Do nothing. Just let the fly swing across unmolested by human activity. It's all right if it drags a little (most trout anglers have trouble with this concept). The intent of this presentation is to move the fly steadily and slowly in front of a steelhead's lie. Changes in speed or direction, or wiggles of the fly while it is swinging will tend to put off the steelhead. What is needed is a slow, steady, infuriating tease.

If your fly drags too much, either cast at more of an angle downstream, or mend line upstream. But don't mend in the middle of the swing unless you can mend well enough to not move the fly (most people aren't good enough menders and should just leave the fly alone).

Maintain a loop of 8-12 inches of line between the reel and your rod

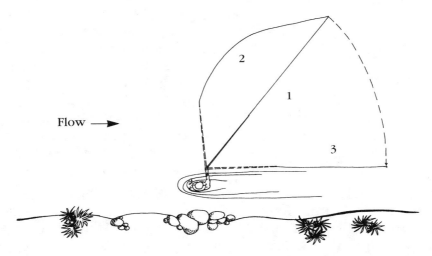

"Classic" steelhead fly presentation. Cast at a 45-degree angle downstream (1), then mend line so as to slow the fly (2), and let the fly swing across the current.

hand. When a fish strikes, the extra friction of the line going through your fingers will help set the hook. Also, you can drop the loop if you have a strike straight downstream (see the next section).

Keep your casting elbow close to your body as the fly swings. This makes the drift steadier, is less tiring, and gives you a chance to thrust the rod toward a fish that takes the fly directly downstream (see next section).

It is important to keep close contact with your fly. Extra loops and coils in your line as it lies on the water diminish the immediacy of that contact. When a steelhead takes the fly, it will hook itself as soon as the line tightens. But if the line is loose, the fish will drop the fly before the line has a chance to tighten up.

Throughout your fly's drift, keep your eye on where you think the fly is (you can't actually see the fly since it is underwater), and stay alert. This kind of fishing is repetitive, and it is easy for you to drift into a torpor and focus your eyes on the middle of the line. But if you do that, you will miss the boils or flashes of fish that you have moved.

Let the fly swing until it is directly below you. Let it hang briefly (maybe five seconds), then slowly strip in about 12 inches of line. Move two or three feet downstream (one step) and cast again.

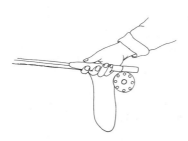

Keeping a loop of line.

When you start a new run, begin casting short—about 20 feet is right in most cases. Lengthen each cast by about three feet until you reach the limits of your good casting distance. Then step downstream before each new cast. This way you will cover the water consistently and methodically.

How Steelhead Move to the Fly. Most steelhead runs in the Deschutes are broad, and the fish are not constrained by ledges and other obstructions. Therefore, when a receptive fish sees a fly, it often follows the fly before taking it. Many times a fish follows the fly until it stops its swing, then the fish hovers there studying it. The angler, unaware of the interested fish, strips in the fly, steps downstream, and plants the next cast past this receptive fish, which has returned to its previous lie.

When you move a fish like this, you can often get it to strike if you know it is there. Another cast in the same place will often induce a strike. Unfortunately, an angler seldom knows that a fish has followed a fly. In fact, many steelheaders, if they knew how often they moved a receptive fish and then passed it by, would give up the sport and sob uncontrollably when anyone mentioned it.

Refer to the illustration of how a steelhead often follows a fly, but does not take it, and the one that shows a typical steelhead take. A few conclusions that can be drawn from these illustrations are:

You rarely hook a steelhead where it was lying.

Pay attention to the water where your fly is. Look for a boil or a flash that indicates a fish that has moved, but not taken.

When your fly stops its swing, let it hang for a moment. Then slowly strip in about 12 inches of line. Give a waiting fish time to grab your fly.

Steelhead will usually hook themselves. When they take the fly and turn to go back to their lie, they pull the fly into the corner of their jaw and hook themselves if your line is tight.

If you strike a fish that has taken your fly when it is straight downstream from you, you will pull the fly out of its mouth. Give it time to close its mouth on the fly and begin moving back to its lie. If you detect

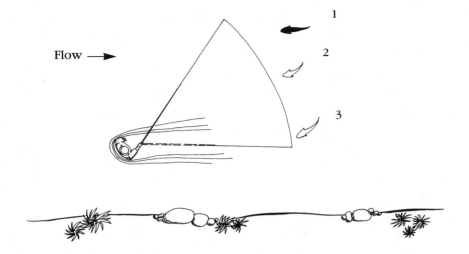

Steelhead following a fly, but not taking it. Fish sees the fly as it passes its lie (1), follows it (2) all the way to the end of the swing and sits there looking at it (3). This fish is a "player" and can probably be hooked IF the angler knows it's there.

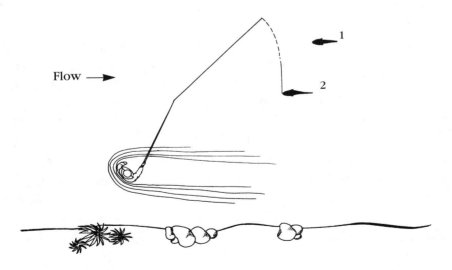

Steelhead taking a fly and returning to its lie. Fish sees the fly as it passes its lie (1), follows it for a ways then grabs it (2). Fish will now return to its lie.

a fish beginning to pull on your fly when it is straight below you, you will need the greatest amount of self-control you have ever exercised in your life. Resist the urge to strike! Instead, drop the loop of line in your hand and push the rod to the fish. This gives the fish some slack so it can close its mouth and start to return to its lie.

Dealing with Plucks and Boils. As discussed in the previous section, steelhead often follow a fly without taking it. When they return to their lie, you might see a flash in the water or a boil behind your fly. Sometimes they will grab at your fly and not get hooked, and you may feel a sudden jerk or a pluck. When you get a strong pluck but no fish, don't despair. You have found a receptive fish and are well on your way to a hook-up.

When you have moved a fish, immediately cast again. If you get no take, cast again, but mend line downstream. This will pull the fly across the steelhead's lie at a faster speed and with a broadside presentation. If there is still no take, walk upstream about ten feet and tie on a new fly. The new fly should be different than the one you were using. The old adage is "smaller and darker," but in the Deschutes it just needs to be different; "bigger and brighter" can work just as well. Come back down on the fish again with the standard cast-step-cast-step tactic. By moving upstream and coming down again you will put a different fly in slightly different places, and this may be enough to induce a strike.

Playing and Landing Steelhead. If you are a beginning steelheader, the first time you hook a fish and it starts to run you may feel completely out of control. A common human reaction is to seize control by grabbing the reel with both hands and your teeth to keep the fish from running away with your fly line. Don't do it! Let the fish run. After the steelhead has run for a while, you might slow it down a little by palming the reel,

> *"Most steelhead fly fishers set the hook too soon or too hard. When you have a take, let the fish take the fly to the point of pulling line off the reel, then swing the rod smoothly and deliberately toward the bank, holding only the cork grip and not the line. This should be enough to set the hook."* John Smeraglio, river guide and owner of the Deschutes Canyon Fly Shop.

but if your drag is properly adjusted, drag alone will wear the fish down. The fish will stop eventually.

Hold your rod so the fish bends it in a deep arc. This makes the fish fight against the rod. Also, hold your rod to the side, rather than pointing it downstream at the steelhead. This puts sideways pressure on the fish and makes it harder for the fish to keep its head pointed into the current. This wears the steelhead down quicker. A fish that is downstream from you, with the rod pointed in its direction, is not going to wear out very fast. On the contrary, you are supporting the fish and letting it rest from the current. So keep the rod partly to the side, or you will be at this all day.

You might want to recover line by walking downstream (very carefully) while reeling in. Keep in mind that steelhead are strong fish and have several good runs in them. They are spooked by shallow water and your presence, so don't think the fight is over the first time you get the fish close to you. Typically, they will come in close, make another run, come in again, then probably run again. You may go through this process several times. Be sensitive to what the fish is doing. When a fish is exhausted it will roll over on its side. This is a good time to pull it towards you.

When you have your steelhead in close, don't pull straight up on it with your rod. A vertical lift will often cause the hook to pull out of the fish. Bring the fish in close by swinging your rod to the side.

When you have your fish in close and can see that it is a wild steelhead, release it in the water. Don't take it out of the river if at all possible. Even one minute in the air can greatly decrease the steelhead's chances of survival.

If it is a hatchery fish and you want to keep it, go ahead and land it. The most common way to land a steelhead is to "tail" it by grabbing it just in front of the tail. Fish are slippery, and a cotton glove or handkerchief on your hand will improve your grip. Another landing method is to slide the fish onto a sandy beach. Unfortunately, there are few steelhead runs on the Deschutes that offer a convenient beaching place.

Tailing a hatchery steelhead.

A few places that should be avoided when landing steelhead that you intend to release are areas of dry rocks or gravel. Pulling a violently flopping fish onto dry, hard, abrasive surfaces like these will remove many of its scales and make it vulnerable to disease after you have released it.

What makes a really good steelhead fly fisher? Why is it that some people consistently catch more steelhead on a fly than other people? A secret run that they fish? Maybe a special fly? The ability to make long casts? I believe it is none of the above. The elements of good steelhead fishing are the ability to read the water and to fish where the fish are, to cast well and in a manner that does not put off the fish, to present the fly in a consistent, steady manner, and to detect a moving (but not taking) steelhead and take advantage of it. These are all little things, yet the really successful anglers do all of these things exceedingly well.

To join their ranks you need to execute each of the above elements consistently, cast after cast. Most people can be pretty good for the first 25 or 30 casts. After that their mind starts to wander, the casts are just a little bit off the mark, the presentation just so-so .

The experts are able to maintain their consistency and keep an almost metaphysical faith that each cast is going to be the one that hooks a fish. Their 500th cast of the day is just as sharp as their first. And many days it takes several hundred good casts to hook one fish. If you don't maintain your edge and your consistency, you may not make several hundred *good* casts in a day . . . and not hook any steelhead.

Fishing for Steelhead with Spinners, Spoons, and Plugs

There is no steelhead apartheid in the Deschutes; there is not one kind of steelhead for fly fishers and another for hardware casters. There is only one type of fish, but they lie in many different types of water. A good angler recognizes all types of steelhead water, and knows where the fish are. But the good angler also understands that some types of tackle are better suited to certain types of steelhead water than are other types of tackle. This angler also realizes that you don't fish all waters the same: you might stand in one place to cast a spoon, but in a different place to cast a spinner to the same fish. However, it is the same species of fish with the same kind of behavior.

About 80 percent of what was said in the section above on fly fishing for steelhead applies to angling with hardware. Hardware fishers should read the above section (and fly fishers should read this one). In particular, the section on playing and landing steelhead applies to all steelhead anglers.

Gear. A light-weight trout rod does not have the backbone needed for these fish, so use a drift rod or spinning rod built for steelhead. Drift rods are better for casting heavy tackle, like drift gear, large casting plugs, and large spoons. On the other hand, spinning rods will do a better job of casting a light weight spinner, especially when the wind starts to blow.

Regardless of your rod choice, keep your reel well lubricated and the drag properly adjusted. Good quality eight pound line is adequate for the Deschutes. Some skilled anglers use six pound line because the lighter line helps the lure get deeper, creates less drag, and gives them a better feel for the lure's action. These anglers also recognize that they are going to lose some fish, and they know that they need to be careful not to overplay their fish, especially when the water is warm.

Either spinners, spoons, or plugs can be used effectively. However, traditional bottom-hugging drift tackle has limited use on the Deschutes. This is because the river bottom is very rocky, and drift gear will frequently be hung up.

Lures. Spinners and spoons used in the Deschutes can be larger and brighter than most people would select for summer-run steelhead. This is because a lot of plant material and other debris flows through the Deschutes in the summer and early fall, making it run slightly off-color. Therefore, many of the traditional guidelines for selecting a summer-run steelhead lure do not apply, since those guidelines assume rivers will run low and clear in summer.

Spinners can be size 3, 4, or even 5. Color is not as critical as in many summer-run rivers, but the best choices are silver, nickel, brass, or black. A size 4 or 5 silver or nickel spinner is fine under almost all conditions on the Deschutes. If the fishing pressure is heavy and the action is slow, try moving to a smaller, darker lure.

A strip of Kelly green tape improves the productivity of silver, nickel, or brass spinners. You can find this tape in some tackle stores. When applying tape to the spinner, put it on the inside (back) of the blade, so the steelhead will see the color from behind the lure (this is the same principle as using a fly with a different colored butt, such as the popular Green Butt Skunk).

Suitable commercial spinners are Mepps Aglia, Blue Fox Vibrax, Metric, and similar brands. However, building your own spinners is easy and much cheaper than buying them. You generally get a better product, too.

The color guidelines for spinners also apply to spoons. Spoons similar to the popular Stee-lee are good producers on this river.

Plugs made for casting by themselves are available. A well-designed plug, cast by a skilled angler, can be fished in a wide range of depths, from shallow to deep. Choose a plug that matches the color of the light reflected by the water where you think the steelhead are: silver in sunny, well-lit water; gold if there is a high overcast; green, blue, or purple on a dark day or in shadows.

Side planers are sometimes used on the Deschutes. Frankly, I can't recommend side planers. I feel they defeat the intent of the "no fishing from boats" rule, require little skill, and are unsporting. For these reasons, they have been outlawed in some areas, like British Columbia. I would like to see them banned on the Deschutes, as well.

Hooks. Hooks are very important on all lures. Many spoons come with a large, single hook. This is very damaging to trout that may pick it up. Replace these big hooks with either a smaller single or treble hook. Round-bend French-style treble hooks are good on all lures because the thinner wire increases the ability to penetrate, and thus increases the chance of a good hook-up.

Recall that all flies and lures on the Deschutes must be barbless, and all wild steelhead must be released unharmed. If a steelhead takes the lure deeply, use wire cutters to cut off the hooks before releasing the fish. If necessary, cut off the entire lure; it will work lose and drop out in a couple of days. Don't stick pliers down the fish's throat and spend a long time twisting and turning the hooks to get them out. Cut them off

> *"The Deschutes is off-colored for most of the summer steelhead season. You can use larger brighter hardware under these conditions because the fish feel more secure."* Jed Davis, author of *Spinner Fishing for Steelhead, Salmon, and Trout,* and owner of Pen Tac, a mail order supplier and manufacturer of spinner and spoon components.

and replace them.

Sharpen your hooks frequently. Most store-bought lures have cheap, dull hooks, and the hooks on all spinners and spoons dull quickly from hitting rocks on the bottom. Many good anglers touch up their hook points every half hour or so.

Recognizing Good Steelhead Hardware Water. Good spinner and spoon water is the same as good fly fishing water (see above). Some of these waters are actually easier to fish with a spoon or spinner than with a fly, especially water that is upstream from the angler, rough water, such as riffles and the heads of runs, and deeper water.

Other good places to fish lures are:

Tailouts—at the end of a run where the bottom rises up in prior to the next riffle.

Drop-offs—where shallow water is abruptly followed by deep water.

Pocket water—small areas around large boulders that may hold only one fish.

While much water can be fished equally well with spinners or spoons, spinners are better suited to shallow, boulder-strewn runs, and spoons are better suited to deep water.

Pay close attention to shallow (two or three feet deep) riffles. In bright light, steelhead often move into this type of water. The white froth and the broken surface gives them a sense of security from predators. In addition, riffle water contains more oxygen, which is critical to the fish when the water warms up. Many anglers by-pass this kind of water, thinking, "why would a big fish rest in shallow, fast water?" In fact, this is some of the best water on the river when the sun is out.

Plugs have an advantage in very deep water because the design of the plug is such that the water forces it down. Here it flutters and vibrates in a steelhead's face and induces a strike. Ask a friend to wiggle his hand back and forth in front of your face, about six inches from your nose. Then you will understand the principle behind fishing a plug, and why a large fish would want to smack the bejabbers out of it.

Hardware Tactics. Anglers using spinners, spoons, and plugs can do very well on the Deschutes. As with all angling techniques, a wide variety of approaches will work if executed well. What is described here are a few basic tactics.

The goal of your presentation is to have your lure working properly

Releasing a wild steelhead. (Courtesy ODFW)

at the right depth when it reaches the fish. For instance, for a spinner you want your lure close to the bottom (usually), moving slowly, and with the blade turning as slowly as possible. When fishing a run, think to yourself, "where are the fish likely to be?" Then cast so the lure has a chance to sink to the proper depth and achieve the right kind of action by the time it reaches the suspected holding places.

A downstream-and-across presentation similar to that for flies (see above) is preferred, but not essential. If possible, position yourself so you can achieve this.

When you are covering a long run with a large lure, such as a large spoon or a size 4 or 5 spinner, each successive cast should be about five feet downstream from the previous one. With a smaller lure, such as a size 3 spinner, successive casts should be three feet apart. When you have covered all the water you can reach from your position, move downstream about ten feet (four or five steps) and do another series of similar casts.

Notice that with this tactic you will be casting into water near where you cast before, but because of factors like retrieval speed and casting distance, you will often be covering fresh water.

Retrieval speed is very important. Spinners and spoons are attractive because they emit pulses of light and vibrations of sound as they spin or wobble. The slower the pulse, the more effective the lure. If your lure is moving fast and is just a blur of light, it is not fishing as well as it could be.

Therefore, retrieve your lure fast enough to keep it off the bottom, but as slow as you can and still give it action. Upstream casts may need a fast retrieve to stay off the bottom and give action, but once the lure is below you, you need to slow your retrieve.

Steelhead sometimes will follow, but not take, a spinner or spoon (as with flies; see above). Therefore, when your lure reaches the end of its swing, reel in slowly for the first 15-20 feet so that a following fish has a chance to follow and grab it.

Good Hardware Fishing. Some hardware anglers walk up to a run, stand on one rock (the same one every time they fish this run), and cast away. They make about 50 casts, most of which land in the same spot, and retrieve their lure at the same speed regardless of where it is in the flow. When the lure has swung all the way across the current, they immediately reel in as fast as they can and cast again. After their 50 casts, they walk away and look for another run. This is not good fishing.

Good fishing covers the water thoroughly, exploring every niche where a fish might lie. Good fishing matches the retrieval speed of the lure to the water it is in at every moment. Good fishing recognizes the needs of steelhead, and works out tactics that are suited to the conditions of that day and hour.

Some fly fishers get snooty about people who use hardware, but an expert hardware fisher is as skilled as an expert fly fisher. Regardless of what approach to steelhead an angler uses, some things stay the same: you need to understand how and why steelhead behave as they do, you need to be able to read the water and adapt your technique to fit different situations, your casts need to be accurate and cover all the fishable water, your presentation has to be flawless, and you need to respect and care for the river resource.

Fishing for Salmon

Steelhead and trout get most of the publicity on the Deschutes. However, there is an active chinook salmon fishery here. It is not as well known because most of the action takes place in a brief six week period and in about one mile of the river. Also, while the Deschutes is a world-class fishery for trout and steelhead, it is only average for salmon.

The salmon muscle their way up river until they get to Sherars Falls. Here, they pool up below the falls where the river is narrow. Most of the fishing happens here because the salmon are so concentrated. Native Americans recognized this concentration of salmon several millennia ago, and have fished at Sherars Falls ever since. They use dip nets and set nets—walking out on precarious wooden platforms to get over the fish——and sport gear.

Salmon regulations for the Deschutes allow sport fishing from April 1 to October 31. In practice, the salmon season is much shorter. By mid-

May, the spring chinook run is over, and recent returns of the fall fish have been so poor that the season is usually canceled. This leaves a six week shot at Deschutes salmon in the spring.

Chinook Salmon. Deschutes chinook salmon average 12-15 pounds, although fish over 30 pounds are sometimes caught. There are two distinct runs of chinook salmon in the Deschutes. The spring run includes both wild and hatchery salmon. Hatchery plants come from the ODFW hatchery at Round Butte, and from the Warm Springs hatchery. This latter hatchery is jointly managed by the federal government and the CTWS. The fall run is entirely wild fish.

Like steelhead, baby salmon stay in the river until they are four or five inches long and smolt. Most migrate to the ocean in the spring, although a few migrate in the fall. If you are catching a lot of small "trout" at these times, they are probably chinook smolts making their run to salt water. Release them carefully; they are a lot more interesting when they come back in a few years.

Returning spring chinook stay in the river until late summer. Adult stocked fish are intercepted at the hatcheries on the Warm Springs River and at Round Butte, but wild spring chinook are allowed to continue their journey and spawn in the Warm Springs River and Shitike Creek. Most fall chinook enter the Deschutes in September, although a few arrive as early as June. They spawn in the main river in October through December. Unlike trout and steelhead, all salmon die after spawning. You can often find their white bodies in the backeddies and shallows in the fall.

About two-thirds of spring chinook that are caught are taken by non-Indian sport fishers. The remaining one-third are taken by Indian netters and sport fishers.

Wild Salmon Management. The native spring chinook salmon are supplemented with hatchery plants. All wild spring salmon spawn in the Warm Springs River and Shitike Creek. The fall run is all wild fish, and they spawn in the main river. The fall run is dangerously weak at this time for reasons that are not clear. Because of these weak runs, the fall chinook sport season has been canceled for several years.

Tackle. Standard drift fishing gear is used: spinning or bait casting reel, medium weight salmon/steelhead rod. Twelve pound line should be sufficient in most cases.

The most common terminal rig is bait (eggs, etc.), with a little yarn

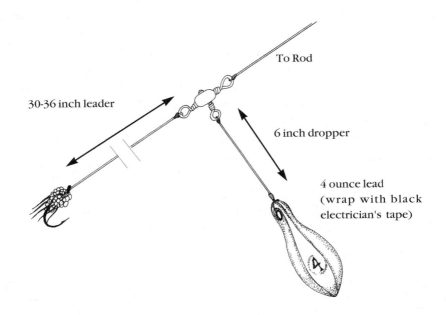

To Rod

30-36 inch leader

6 inch dropper

4 ounce lead
(wrap with black
electrician's tape)

and a spin-and-glo or corkie in peach or green colors. Use about three feet of leader and a four-ounce sinker on a dropper, as shown. Most people wrap the sinker with electrician's tape. This keeps the soft lead sinker from being gouged as it is reeled in past the rocky banks. Gouges in the lead can nick the monofilament line and weaken it.

Closer to the falls the current is much stronger, and large cannon ball sinkers (16 ounces or more) are used. This requires a much stouter rod.

As with everywhere else on the river, you may only use barbless hooks, and you may not fish from a floating device. Bait may be used from Sherars Falls to a point about three miles downstream from the falls. However, most of the fishing takes place at the falls themselves because the salmon are concentrated there.

Tactics. Hopeful anglers gather near Sherars Bridge and fish from the high banks downstream from the falls. The banks are solid basalt and drop straight to the river, a distance of from 10 to 30 feet. If you get vertigo, don't fish here!

Cast upstream, and let your rig sink to the bottom. As it comes back to you, reel in line so your sinker is bouncing on the bottom, but the line is tight enough so you can detect a take. As the line comes past you, either let out some line so it drifts downstream in the current, or walk downstream with it. When your rig has swung across the current, reel in and cast again.

When a salmon takes the bait, it will feel like your rig has just stopped. Strike hard. If it is a fish, it will pull back. Otherwise, you are probably hung up on a rock. If your rig drifts into a backeddy, you may hook a squawfish, whitefish, or chiselmouth. This will test your character more than your tackle.

Because anglers, like salmon, are concentrated in a small area at Sherars Falls, it is easy to cross lines and snag another fisherman's rig. If one angler hooks a salmon, all other anglers need to reel-in immediately and get out of the way. Usually another angler will climb down to the water at one of the few access points and net the fish. In one area, the person netting the fish has to climb down a 30-foot ladder, then come back up again carrying the fish!

Fishing for salmon at Sherars is not for everyone. This is crowded, "meat" fishing, and there is a fraternity aspect to it. For the uninitiated, the unwritten rules may seem hard to determine. If you do something wrong, people may just look at you like you're an idiot while you wonder what on earth you did.

If you are unfamiliar with the etiquette of salmon fishing at the falls, watch other fisherman for a while so you get a feeling for how it's done. Ask someone else about how to do it. If you want more solitude, remember that you can use bait for three miles below Sherars Falls.

10

Services

Your boat trailer breaks a weld on the rough Deschutes access roads. Who do you call? Your drift boat sinks in Whitehorse rapids. Who do you call? You need a place to stay, a shuttle, 25 box lunches for the office whitewater trip, and you have a toothache in Maupin. Who do you call?

Here is a brief guide to services you might need while in the Deschutes River area. Some specific services are listed, and there is an overview of what to expect in nearby towns. Because Maupin is in the heart of the lower Deschutes area and has the greatest concentration of services for the recreationist, there is a complete list of relevant businesses in Maupin. Unless stated otherwise, all these businesses are on US 197 (the main street in Maupin) and are in the central business area.

When using this chapter, keep in mind that new businesses will have started after this book is published, so some services will be available that are not listed here. Likewise, some that are listed here may change their hours, change their locations, or even go on to other endeavors.

Services in Maupin

Lee Balentine, DDS. Dentist. Open 9-6, Monday through Friday. 395-2636. Emergencies: 395-2594.

B&H Cafe and Pizza. Cafe. Pizza, sandwiches, fountain, "slushees." Open 8-6, 7 days a week all year.

Barnett Service. Gas, automotive repair, welding, 24 hour towing. Open 8-6, 7 days a week in summer; closed Sundays in winter (November-April). 395-2543. Night emergency towing: 395-2413.

CJ Lodge. Bed and breakfast on river. Located on the east side of the river near City Park on the way to the north access road. Private entry, private bath. From $55 per night. Teepees at $7 per person, shower and sleeping pad included. Guided whitewater raft trips, 1-3 days. Fishing guide service can be arranged. Shuttle parking and showers following trips. Showers available to the public for $2.00 per person. 395-2404.

City Park. Located on the east side of the river just north of the bridge. In addition to camping, which is described in Chapter 5, the Maupin City Park has a community building with kitchen. This can be rented by groups.

Columbia River Bank. Open Monday, Wednesday, Friday 11-4. Twenty-four hour cash machine near main door accepts Cirrus, Visa, Plus, and Cash 24.

Community Church. Located on a side street just off the central business district. 9AM worship, 10:30 Sunday School, 6PM worship.

Deschutes Canyon Fly Shop/Green Drake Gallery. Located just west of the bridge. Complete fly fishing store and wildlife art gallery. Orvis and Courtland Pro shop. Guided walk-in fly fishing trips, casting lessons. March through October, open 8AM-6PM Monday-Sunday, closes later Friday and Saturday. November through February, open 10AM-4PM Friday through Sunday; or call anytime. 395-2565.

Deschutes Motel. Located just west of town. 12 unit motel. All units have private bath, 4 units have kitchenettes. $30 and up per night. Open all year. 395-2626.

Deschutes River Adventures. Raft rental from $55. Delivery and pick-up of rafts. Guided one day and overnight trips. Some fishing tackle, flies, bait (during salmon season), gifts, ice. Boater's passes, shuttles. Open 9-6, Monday-Friday; 8-6, Saturday and Sunday. Closed October-March. 1-800-RAFTING.

Deschutes River Inn. Restaurant serving breakfast, lunch, dinner. Catering for river groups and box lunches available. Open 6AM-9PM, 7 days a week all year. Closes a little later in summer. 395-2468.

Deschutes U-Boat. Located just east of the bridge. Raft rental. Over 80 rafts of various sizes. Delivery and pickup of rafts to launch sites. One day or overnight guided trips. Shuttles, boater's passes, snacks, drinks, sundries. Open 8-6, Monday to Friday; 7-10, Saturday and Sunday. Closed November through March. 395-2503.

Deschutes Whitewater Services. Located on the east side of the main business district. Raft rentals. Guided white water trips, half day to three days. Delivery and pick up of rafts. Will supply lunches for one day trips. Boater's Passes, shuttles. 395-2232.

Desert Rose Bed and Breakfast. Located at the east end of the business district. Bed and breakfast in quaint, renovated 1920s house with period furniture. Two rooms with double beds, $75 per night per person. Oriented to anglers, with breakfasts/brunches scheduled dependent on when the best fishing happens. Fly fishing guide service can be arranged. 395-2662.

Ewing's Whitewater. Guided whitewater or fishing trips. 1-5 days. Can custom design trips to accommodate large groups, elderly, handicapped, etc. Cater quality food for customers. 800-538-7238.

Graves Market. Grocery and liquor store. Fresh meat and produce. Open 8-7, 7 days a week all year. May close a little earlier in winter. 395-2234.

Kaufmann's Fly Fishing Expeditions, Inc. House on the east side of the bridge, at the beginning of the south access road. Guided fly fishing trips for trout and steelhead. Fly fishing schools. Overnight lodging for those enrolled in schools or multi-day trips. 639-6400 or 800-442-4359 for reservations.

Koviashuvik (an Eskimo word meaning "a time and place of peace and joy in the present moment"). Variety store, including gifts, art, video rental, books, music, gourmet coffee beans. The Visitor's Center is also here. 395-2233.

Maupin Laundromat. Coin-operated 24 hour laundromat.

Maupin Medical Center. Open Tuesdays and Fridays 9AM-noon.

Rapid River Rafters. 1-2-3 day guided paddle trips in self bailing rafts. Last minute reservations welcome. 395-2545.

Rainbow Tavern. Food and drinks. Steak feed Friday nights from 5-10. Open 11AM-10PM weekdays, 11 to midnight on Fridays and Saturdays. 395-2962.

Redsides Building Supply. General hardware, some fishing tackle and camping supplies. Fishing licenses, Boater's Passes. Open 8-5 all year; closed Sundays. 395-2217.

Richmond Service. Gas station, automotive repair, welding. Open 8-6 all year; closed Sundays. 395-2638.

Riverside Hotel. Located just east of the bridge. Hotel, restaurant, lounge. Rooms from $19. Restaurant open 6AM-10PM April through November; 11AM-10PM December through March. Live music in lounge on Friday and Saturday nights, April through December 15.

River Trails Rafting. Located on the east side, on the way to the north access road. Raft rentals. Delivery and pickup of rafts. $45 per day and up. Boater's passes, shuttles. Can arrange guided trips. Also have an outlet in Troutdale. 395-2545.

St. Mary Catholic Church. Corner of Burnham and Dufur Streets. Mass first and third Sundays at 10:30AM, Communion service second and fourth Sundays at 10:30AM.

The Oasis Resort. Located on the east side of the river shortly after the bridge. Cafe and motel. Open 8AM-10PM, Monday-Thursday; 8AM-11PM Friday; 6AM-11PM Saturday; 6AM-10PM Sunday. Ten rooms, 4 with kitchenettes; $25-$48. Gas. Guided fishing trips for trout or steelhead. Parking, shuttles, boater's passes, fishing tackle, gifts. Closed November-March. 395-2611.

Wild Water River Company. Guided whitewater and fishing trips, half day to overnight. Some raft rentals. Shuttles, boater's passes. 395-2257.

White Water Pictures. Located on the east side on the way to the north access road. Takes photos of every craft running Box Car rapids, seven days a week from mid-June through Labor Day, and weekends May through September. Takes photos in Oak Springs rapids on weekends during same period. Contact sheets of photos on display at shop; examine there and order prints. Also have yogurt and ice cream at shop.

Services in Other Towns

Biggs. Biggs is at the junction of US 97 and I-84. It is a small community offering what you would expect at a highway junction: gas stations and a scattering of motels, restaurants, and mini-marts. Dinty's Market-Deli has some fishing tackle.

Dufur. Dufur is an agricultural community, but it has a few services of interest to river users: a hardware store, grocery, restaurants, and the

Balch Hotel, a recently renovated facility in a historic 19th century brick building.

Madras. Madras is one of the largest towns in the area and offers many services such as restaurants, motels, and gas stations. There are two fishing tackle stores in Madras. Oscar's Sporting Goods, 380 SW 5th, has a complete supply of fishing tackle, including fly fishing gear. Madras Gun and Tackle, 1810 Highway 97, also has fishing tackle, including fly gear and fly tying supplies.

The Dalles. The Dalles (that's not "Dallas", and don't forget the "The") is a large town of 11,000 people. It has many amenities and services, including two fishing tackle stores: Homer's Sporting Goods (908 E. 2d) and Young's Sporting Goods (515 E. 2d). Both carry hard tackle and trout and steelhead flies. Young's also has fly tying materials.

Tygh Valley. Tygh Valley is a very small community with a general store and a cafe.

Warm Springs. The town of Warm Springs is the headquarters for the Confederated Tribes of Warm Springs (CTWS). There are several services on US 26 near the town, including gas stations and cafes. The Rainbow Market, which is near the boat ramp just south of the bridge (and hence not on the Reservation), has some groceries, Boater's Passes, and Warm Springs permits. A CTWS museum opened in 1993; it is on US 26.

Welches. Welches is on US 26 west of Mt. Hood. The Fly Shop, located in the shopping center on US 26, is a complete fly tackle dealer with quality equipment, fly tying material, and guide service for the Deschutes. They open at 7AM to accommodate Deschutes-bound fly fishers.

Fishing Guides

There are almost 200 guides who operate in some fashion on the Deschutes, although there are only a handful that are full-time fishing guides on the river. The Deschutes River Public Outfitters can direct you to a fishing guide. Call them at 800-952-0707.

Shuttles

Some drivers shuttle the entire river, others only near their home base. All phone numbers are area code 503.

Madras

Farrell's Shuttle Service 475-2825
Fish Shuttle Service 475-6009
Gayle Rodgers 475-3966
Marcia Buck 475-7532
Oscar's Sporting Goods 475-2962
Steckley's Shuttle Service 475-3129

Maupin

Deschutes River Adventures 1-800-RAFTING
Deschutes River U-Boat 395-2503
Deschutes Whitewater Services 395-2232
The Oasis 395-2611
Wild Water River Company 395-2257

The Dalles

Bob Paulsen 296-1250
Dave Urban 296-4982
River Runner Shuttle Service 298-4004

Raft and Drift Boat Rental

If you intend to rent a raft or drift boat, call in advance for a reservation, and give them time to set it up for you.

Deschutes River Adventures (Maupin) 1-800-RAFTING
Deschutes U-Boat (Maupin) 395-2503
Deschutes Whitewater Services (Maupin) 395-2232
Drift Boat Rental (Gateway) 475-3966
River Trails Rafting (Maupin) 395-254.

Whitewater Trips

Some outfitters can take you at the last minute, but it is always a good idea to arrange your trip in advance. Just about every rafting contractor in the Northwest runs trips on the Deschutes. The ones listed here are some of the primary providers.

Deschutes River Adventures 1-800-RAFTING
Deschutes U-Boat 395-2503
CJ Lodge 395-2404
Deschutes Whitewater Services 395-2232
Rapid River Rafters 395-2545
Ewing's Whitewater 395-2697
Hunter Expeditions 389-8370

Emergencies

Throughout the Deschutes area, you can dial 911 for police, medical, and fire emergencies.

White Water Salvage in Redmond is the place to call for serious river salvage problems (like sinking the boat in a rapids or wrapping the raft around a rock). Mark Angel, long-time salvage expert on the Deschutes will help you. 923-0124.